D1320214

Ten Commandments
for the Long Haul

JOURNEYS IN FAITH

Creative Dislocation—The Movement of Grace
Robert McAfee Brown

Speech, Silence, Action!
Virginia Ramey Mollenkott

Hope Is an Open Door
Mary Luke Tobin

By Way of Response
Martin E. Marty

Ten Commandments for the Long Haul

Daniel Berrigan

Journeys in Faith
Robert A. Raines, Editor

ABINGDON

Nashville

TEN COMMANDMENTS FOR THE LONG HAUL

Copyright © 1981 by Abingdon

All rights reserved.

Library of Congress Cataloging in Publication Data

BERRIGAN, DANIEL.
    Ten commandments for the long haul.
    (Journeys in faith)
    I. Christian life—Catholic authors. 2. Berrigan, Daniel. I. Title.
    II. Series.
    BX2350.2.B428   248.4   81-1463   AACR2
                ISBN 0-687-41240-4

Scripture quotations are from the Revised Standard Version of the Bible,
copyrighted 1946, 1952, © 1971, 1973 by the Division of Christian Education
of the National Council of the Churches of Christ in the U.S.A., and are used
by permission.

MANUFACTURED BY THE PARTHENON PRESS AT
NASHVILLE, TENNESSEE, UNITED STATES OF AMERICA

To Lewis, Bob, Fred,
good friends and brothers

Contents

EDITOR'S FOREWORD.................................9

I. RESPONSIBILITIES:
   A DIARY OF SORTS................................. 13

II. TEN COMMANDMENTS FOR THE
    LONG HAUL................................. 76

   1. Love Your Enemies,
     Love One Another.................................76
   2. Do This in Remembrance of Me.............80
   3. Sell What You Possess............................. 86
   4. Do Not Be Afraid................................. 93
   5. When You Are Haled into Court,
     Prepare No Defense.................................97

6. Let Him Who Is Without Sin . . . Be the First to Throw a Stone......................106
7. Lazarus, Come Forth.............................. 112
8. Compel Them to Come In.....................118
9. Flee...121
10. Go, Teach.....................................125

III. A DIALOGUE WITH MY SOUL
ON WHAT I TAKE TO BE THE
HEART OF THE MATTER....................... 131

IV. OF PRIESTS, WOMEN, WOMEN PRIESTS,
AND OTHER UNLIKELY
RECOMBINANTS.....................................139

V. FINALLY—I PLEDGE ALLEGIANCE
TO FORTY-SEVEN GRAFFITI:
A DECLARATION OF DEPENDENCE... 154

Editor's Foreword

People inside and outside the church today are engaged in a profound revisioning of the faith journey. Wanting to honor our own heritage and to be nourished by our roots, we also want to discern the signs of the kingdom now, and to move into the 1980s with a lean, biblical, ecumenical, and human faith perspective.

The *Journeys in Faith* series is offered to facilitate this revisioning of faith. Reflecting on the social justice openings of the 1960s and the inward searching of the 1970s, these books articulate a fresh integration of the faith journey for the years ahead. They are personal and social. Authors have been invited to share what has been happening to them in their faith and life in recent years, and to focus on issues which have become primary for them in this time.

We believe that these lucidly written books will be widely used by study groups in congregations, seminaries, colleges, renewal centers, orders, and denominations, as well as for personal study and reflection.

Our distinguished authors embody a diversity of experience and perspective which will provide many points of identification and enrichment for readers. As we enter into the pilgrimages shared in these books, we will find resonance, encouragement, and insight for a fresh appropriation of our faith, toward personal and social transformation.

In a time when "the American ethos swamps the gospel," Daniel Berrigan has written a book for those who do not want to be overcome. It is a book about the shaping of a confessing or resisting church. It is a book about a minority or remnant church which is willing to pay the costs of saying No to Caesar as the way today to reap the joy of saying Yes to Christ.

It is disconcerting to find a man taking the commandment "Thou shalt not kill" so seriously and directly. Indeed, Berrigan writes, not about options or suggestions, but about *commandments*. One supposes that the Bible crept into his bones early on. It is a *biblical* hopefulness which is cast against the looming cloud of nuclear holocaust. He does not offer an effective strategy. He sounds a call to faithfulness.

If, as Berrigan says, young seminarians need a taste of a good church, many of us need a taste of a good disciple. Berrigan gives us such a taste. From his early renunciation for the life of a Jesuit, not without tears, to his passionate commitment to peacemaking in the troubled places of the world, Berrigan's pilgrimage moves to the marrow. The reader is reminded of other faithful journeys recorded in Hebrews 11 and 12. Berrigan is fiercely constant in his commitment to the "foolishness of peacemaking." This enduring witness over many years sounds through the variations of his ministry like the bass line of a Bach fugue. Berrigan is a man for the long haul. His word and deed are very nearly in focus. There is little left over in the person or the politics. What you see is what you get—a man to be reckoned with. His lover's quarrel with his church and order offers comfort to others struggling with their own faith communities. His mentors are Gandhi, Merton, Martin King. His colleagues are the company of fools for Christ anywhere in the world. He is most at home with the poor and the oppressed, and with those who seek to share their sufferings. His worship is public. He connects the body and the Word, the altar and the Pentagon. He embodies revolutionary patience.

Berrigan writes with rare imagination and leanness of language. Deep, dense, outrageous colors. Unmistakable simplicity of truth.

This is a book to rouse a generation. It rings with gospel hope.

Robert A. Raines

I

Responsibilities:
A Diary of Sorts

1

Slowly, fitfully, during these years I am coming to understand what my life can offer—in word, act, attitude.

I must obey rhythms which neither America nor I can set in motion, or cancel out.

To speak of the inner life, I have said to others: "You cannot long survive in America without something better than America for resource" (I say this first of all to myself).

Call it a tradition, a discipline of prayer, sacrament, the old words and realities worn smooth as David's pebbles. Palm them, press them, fling them. They will save your life, your sanity.

People listened, or tried to. But the violent or lulling waves of the seventies flung them about. What are we to do? Where are we going? Or worse—a cry, "Come and save us!" I took it as a cry of despair.

They would ask, in calmer moments: "How do we become activists?"

My mood at that point was not far removed from their despair that, in the first place, put the wrong query. I would reply, with some heat: "But that is not the question at all. Here's a better one: 'Can we uncover the contemplative springs that are the source of our humanity?'"

Can we clear the waters of our soul, that the streams may run free? This Zen trust in nature—first nature to be sure, undestroyed, uninhibited, unpolluted—can we discover it, allow it scope and free play?

◁ ○ ▷

This was the gift of Thomas Merton, as I came to know him. His life put first things first, so that, indeed, secondary things might also be respected, firmly and gently in place. Thus, he touched both worlds, first and second. Both natures, first and second. Source and consequence, soul and outreach.

Our long, vagrant, unplanned, hilarious, and infinitely precious friendship! There he stood in workman's shoes, firmly and fittingly, in muddy shoes, a workman and a contemplative. Stood there, as one photo shows him, before his hermitage. Like Blake's creative genius, touching all points, world within, world without, world above and beneath, his clear gaze dissolving it all, his cry like that of a Pirandello character: "Reality! reality!"

◁ ○ ▷

It does not exhaust the case to say, Merton showed us the future (though he did that, too, it was his "second world of time").

In a biblical sense, he moved through life with such ease and courage and persistence that he dissolved the out-in impasse. He kicked the Bomb over with his workman's shoes: it had no power over him.

◁ ○ ▷

His achievement goes largely unseen, more than ten years after his death. That achievement being a matter incomprehensible to the world or the worldly church. Thus, in proportion as death is courted, life dreaded, and persistent conscience shunned, Merton remains twice buried. Church and state look on him as they do on Martin King, gingerly and at distance, making great effort to assimilate him. I note how persistently his writings on peace are ignored, and his writing on something they choose to call "spirituality" (a word of which Bible and tradition are alike ignorant) is drawn energetically, gingerly, out of all context.

◁ ○ ▷

What a price he paid to do the simplest Christian thing; see with his eyes, reason with his mind, say what he saw.

Only a few friends knew what he was enduring, only a few walked to the wall. A few stood there with him in silence, bowed before the impasse. There was nothing to be done, he believed, but to stand there, there was nothing for his friends to do (because this was his decision) but to stand there with him, the peacemaker.

This was called obedience, a word scalding to the tongue, his and mine. But a word which purified, like the coal of Isaiah, the one who heard it and stood by it.

In them a vice, a blindness: in him, a virtue transforming.

◁ ○ ▷

He obeyed, as few know. Then he died, as all the world knows. He was taken from us in winter of '68, at the point of our greatest crisis: Catonsville, where nine of us burned draft records with home-made napalm in May of 1968. After that death, it seemed there could be nothing further to suffer. In him, we lost everything that could be lost, short of our own life. Or so it seemed at the time, and for a long time after.

Then, death having done its worst, healing started. Gradually, I folded that loss, monstrous as it seemed (and was, and is) in the coda of loss and gain which governs the dance of the universe. To include that loss, even as a gain; Merton, friend, advocate in a better court: one who stood at our side, and would forever.

But the wound was there, only thinly healed over.

We went on alone, my friends and I who were also Merton's friends, into the vortex of the late sixties, court, underground, jail.

But that story is told elsewhere.*

2

We survived prison, came out on our feet, my brother married, Jonah House came into being. It was to be a focal point of our lives for the next decade.

Specifically, in forging resistance against nuclear weapons, and this at a time when very few seemed ready to face the Armageddon then (and now) in preparation.

The record of that house, and the community that came and went, grew and declined and grew again, has yet to be told. In the decade of the Long and Lugubrious Sleep, the people of Jonah House kept watch, were "alert to the signs of the times." They were arrested innumerable times, maintained presence at the Pentagon and the Blight House, traveled about the country speaking of nuclear realities on campus, in churches, wherever they could gain a hearing.

Internally, the house was marked by clarity of outlook, fervent purpose and discipline. It started as an experiment in faith: it remains so, with prayer and sacrament at the heart of its effort. For many of us who lived and worked elsewhere, the community was a land and sea mark; there we took soundings and found direction; we joined in its struggle, its members were the best friends of our lives.

I took up teaching once more, at Union Seminary in New York, the University of Manitoba, Detroit University, Yale, Berkeley. But the best year of all I spent in a cul-de-sac in the South Bronx, that area of blight and broken promise. There, as may be recalled, Jimmy Carter showed his untrue mettle, first by

*The Dark Night of Resistance (Doubleday, Bantam); Prison Poems (Unicorn, Viking); Lights On in the House of the Dead (Doubleday); Absurd Convictions, Modest Hopes (Random House)

walking its lunar rubble, then by proceeding to ignore and deny what he had there affirmed. For there were other more pressing interests at stake: his political survival, the clamorous generals, the Shah and his oil, the juntas, the languishing economy, Kennedy's hot breath at his shoulder. . . .

It was a season of betrayal, a season a decade long. The earth languished, the storms lashed, the rich grew richer, the poor dropped out of the world. There was not even an outcry. Our city was being reduced before our eyes to a public ward crowded with amputees, the mute, the blind, the halt, the unhinged: casualties all. There was less of everything, crime excepted. New York was beaten to its knees by voracious banks and corporations, who thereupon briskly proceeded to take control of the emergency room.

As of today, they remain in control. We are told by impeccable authority that both the governor and the mayor have a guru, confidant. In each case, the privileged ear belongs to a banker.

◁ ○ ▷

It was a bad time to test one's vision.

Or was it a good time, the times that would show the true face of vision—or its false face?

I reflected: what was a "good time" anyway? One could scarcely imagine a "good time": it seemed more and more like a mirage, receding as one went toward it. I thought wryly: one knew well enough what bad times were, one tasted them and heard them and smelled them and took them in at the pores. But what could "good times" mean? One could scarcely imagine. Versions were thrust at us out of the tube, out of polluted movies, out of department store windows, all showing their wares, the smirk of a pimp, the hip of a whore. Good times were the crazed, insatiable appetites that, like the craw of a monstrous bird, grew on what they fed on.

The vision could not depend on the times. The vision had to depend on itself, and the people who were willing to work and sweat and suffer and hear the doors lock behind them, as sweet liberty took flight through the barred window, a dove in full retreat.

3

All that traipsing about the world saying my say, all those audiences, those overnight stops, those campuses affluent and sleep-ridden, those airports that freeze the soul, those night buses (the dark-bellied Leviathans, their sleeping prey), those autos, dangerous and foolish hands at the wheel, those near-deaths on speedways. . . .

What did it all mean? Or was the very question a cliché, there being no answer that could win the sensible mind, a key, a commanding voice? I was dumb as a beginner's tongue. I had no equipment to ask such a question. There was only the task to be done; the meaning of the task, if it were well done, done to the best of one's energies and ability and passion—there lay all the meaning that could be reasonably sought. I never paused to ask (and will by no means ask here) something like this—What is the meaning of my life? or indeed, does my life have meaning at all?

I think one part of the American soul has been denied my soul. I lack the cog or sprocket or bolt that would set such questions in motion. Either that, or a merciful hand has turned off a switch somewhere in the universe (somewhere in me) and the part in question no longer functions. It has not functioned since the beginning, since that time when my life first occurred to me, a given, a splendor and darkness, but also a voice, warning: proceed with caution.

It seemed to me that whatever reason could be adduced for staying on my feet in a mad time—this would be granted precisely in the course of the struggle. I could not take my lead, in so crucial a matter as self-knowledge, from the media, hot or cold, from being the darling of the culture, or its political priest (odious phrase) or its saint—or its victim or fall guy. None of these. (Even though I have been cast in each of these absurd and tempestuous roles.)

What had such roles to confer on me after all? Nothing (or near it), or worse—a false sense of myself, my work. I could be loaded with honors or loaded with opprobrium; only to be plunged into a mad market where souls go cheap, the souls of slaves.

◁ ○ ▷

A member of my community would ask of me, on return from this or that junket, this or that audience: And how did things go?

I would find myself mute. And would commonly be misunderstood as indifferent to the bond and concern of my brothers.

By no means indifferent. But suffering the loss or dysfunction of that part, which, had it been humming away, would beyond doubt enable me to declare, bright of eye, and expansive of gesture: "Fine! Terrific! How they were moved! Gales of laughter, buckets of tears! They vowed to change their lives, in accord with the hundred fifty-nine rules of the perfect Tao! They wanted to make me King! Pope! Police chief! I multiplied bread and circus tickets and, thereupon, had to flee to the hills!"

Alas, the lost part, its lost art. Whether its name be ego or charisma or profile or theological chic or saleable image—the sorry fact is, it is missing, or if it is present, it has fallen to misuse, dysfunctional.

What indeed was there to report about public performance? In such times, what could one say? Could ego stroking, self-satisfaction be a sensible state of mind, while public madness proceeded unchecked, while one's best efforts, one's very life and years, were set against an onrushing sea? What place could there be for self-congratulation in a toppling world, an unspeakable and all but inimaginable crime in preparation, the destruction of the human venture and future?

One did one's best, and went on. I did my best, I put the public evenings behind me; the crowds, large or miniscule, melted away, thoughtful or errant as the case might be. One collected his notes, briefly recalled and regretted some flash of anger, impatience, the medium unworthy of the message; and closed the book. Closed the trip, which, within a week or so, melded with every other trip, every other audience, a calendar date turned over.

But that was not the whole story. If it were, if in my own estimate or conviction that were all, I would be little more than a variant of that vagrant deceiving image that is one's "public image."

This was not the whole story: a message, an evening, a calendar date, indistinguishable faces, blurred memories. Not by any means. For the travel was the very journey of my soul. It bore along with it the moral weight of life itself, it sought to create like minded, disciples, opposite numbers. It sought to discharge the hot essence of vision, to make available the weight and weightlessness of an endangered glory, the glory of the human, its grace, its cry, the unstickable will to survive.

Thus, I sensed, almost as a matter of course, a profound rapport and response, a lowering of the guard, some who would listen, a few who would be my friends.

◁ ○ ▷

And as the years went by, friends sprang up everywhere, they appeared out of audiences in any city I entered: "You won't remember me" (I did remember, invariably) "but I met you so many years ago, on such and such an occasion, and I want you to know that this or that word" (or book, or article, or action) "meant such and such to me." (A moral change of some moment, a step taken, freedom grasped, resistance undertaken.) "So, I wanted to thank you."

These were the moments that counted, the past like a moral miracle, a loaf in the right hands, always multiplied. Yesterday's bread fresh for the hunger of today.

And this kept one going.

But such moments could not easily be described, at least by me. In themselves they were without ego or recompense. I can compare them only to the act of love; they were secret and charged with life, undeserved, a grace. But if one were avaricious, lingered over them, laid them out for consumption, they lost their aura, their bouquet. Is there a kind of "moment dropping" which, like name dropping, makes hay of spun gold?

◁ ○ ▷

One newsman asked, undoubtedly seeking a new twist on a stale pretzel: "What words would you want inscribed on your tombstone?" I said, gnawing my pretzel: "May he never rest in peace."

I meant something beyond a joke. In such times as ours, the ego takes its proper measure, not from something so vulgar as crowd appeal, but from the struggle inherent in life itself. If, indeed, the ego is not to stagnate, or lord it over, or utterly give up before the brutal and gargantuan and sinister shape of life.

◁ ○ ▷

This character, his phiz all but hidden in his beard, and leaning forward as though top-heavy from living in his top-story, and speaking so slowly one had the impression every tenth word was making it to his tongue: "Now wotta yew think . . . if somebodies like the Beatles . . . was to get it down with us . . . in this yere movement . . . wouldn't we git . . . near a millyun folk inthestreets. . . ." It was the old Californian "social change through show biz" routine. I mumbled some feeble exit line and made my exit. Like pronto, man.

◁ ○ ▷

Learning to believe. Coming before each audience as I would come before my own soul; this must be the understanding, if all this talk and travel were to be something more than mere show biz.

Audiences, so devouring and constant a part of my life.

Was I ever alone? Was I ever to be alone?

But I was constantly alone, if only I would make the most of opportunity. There was a "being with," there was a "turning around": and both were the gestures of the soul, its dance, assent and refusal.

I could sense a mile away where things were out of kilter, where I was being used, or invaded, or worked over. There is a rising ruff along the back of some animals, they say. I have one, too.

When someone is trying to abuse you, and the ruff rises straight up, it is important to remember; the abusive one is also the abused one. I am not responsible for every form of abuse in the world, especially the abuse of abusive women. But I can be conscious of this and compassionate toward them.

◁ ○ ▷

They ask me sometimes, and mean well by it, "How often have you been arrested?" But I dislike the numbers game, and turn the question aside with: "As yet, not enough."

Which is also the truth, given the times. And my proclivity is to pay as I ride.

They also ask frequently: "Where does your hope come from, how do you keep going?" Which seems to me a serious question, but composed out of insufficient evidence, a question having about it a certain immodest aura, which I'm being invited to stand under. (Should one stand under a light he did not kindle?) I like Philip's typically laconic answer: "Your hope is where your ass is."

As in the case, I judge, of those who sit in. Or in another version: "Your hope is where your feet are" (as in the case of those who march). But hardly ever, in my experience, is one's hope where his head is. Passing strange, to think of it, that those whose heads are presumably screwed on straight, should ask me, "Where is your hope today?"

Passing strange, and strangely true. Hope dwells in the posterior, or in the hands and feet. But hardly ever in that noblest of human members, whose functions, we are told, are to speculate and ponder and envision and calculate and predict and do all those things named by us, properly human. But in fact, so tragically and often: improperly inhuman.

◁ ○ ▷

A double sense of myself, a double bind?

On the one hand, I'm watchful and edgy as Conrad's mad courier, a bomb wired to his body. I expect the "end," I hope for a good end. On the other hand, I'm totally ignorant, have a sense of bearing a skull full of darkness.

Now all this may result now and then in good work, striking or helpful conscientious activity. But when I speak about my work, the words tend to falter, droop on the vine.

Maybe this is close to the Buddhist mind. You do what you do. But what it may mean to others, what direction it takes, this is strictly in others' hands.

So, I lead my life, I follow my nose. But I seldom know what to make of it all. I believe, but I don't know what the world thinks of my belief. (Nor, if truth were told, do I much care.)

Believe it or not, this incapacity and blankness results in a teaching method. I ruminate aloud. I may have a few notes, generally indecipherable. Then the spate opens, especially if I've had a cup of coffee, or fasted ahead of time. The class turns into a kind of interior monologue going outward.

Now figure that out, I can't.

Sometimes a student will interrupt: "What did you just say, I didn't get it."

I answer in all truth: "I don't know what I just said."

"Then will you repeat the gist of it?"

In that case, I fetch about to recover the drift, now and then paraphrase satisfactorily.

It's quite improvised, like life itself. The advantage of my non-method (there are very few advantages) is that I'm not caught in the fly trap of competence and expertise, which I find sterile and suffocating.

This non-method (which I hereby name "serious gaming") is all one can bring to a given situation, teaching, lecturing. I bring to these, not this or that lofty thought or formula or solution—but my life: the stream and headwaters and source, the residue and juice. All of it coming down, the debris, the purity, the accretions, the latest storm, the sunlight warm on water, currents hot and cold. A conscientious awareness and conviction, which can be offered quite modestly; not hustling, merely presenting.

Gandhi seems to have commended this: the truth has its own power, he insists, don't get in the way. Or the Buddhists: Respect the dharma, don't clog things in their course.

Such admonitions shed light on the text I worry around the room, like a dog a bone.

Don't get in the way. If you stand to one side, the text, like a pure stream, will make its way toward you, flow through and through. You might even become, like the wondrous creatures of the Apocalypse, "full of eyes."

4

A proffer was made to me in 1973, to spend a semester in Canada teaching at the University of Manitoba.

A few words of explanation are in order here. I am often at odds with the religious departments of universities; likewise with seminaries. I find the incumbents ordinarily far removed from the realities of life, fervently bent on extrapolating favorite theories, fervently attached to perquisites, marvelously ignorant or indifferent to the plight of people.

All this does not make for a *communitas intellectus*. At Winnipeg, I found myself in the company of nine or ten world experts in world religions. These eminent divines, gathered from the four corners of the globe, held forth on the convergence and branchings of world symbols, ecstatic writings, moral codes, mimes and stories, historic and mystic developments that comprise the rich legacy of the world tribe.

I shall put a painful matter shortly. As time passed, I grew less impressed with my peers; and it became clear that the sentiment was heartily mutual.

Then a breakdown occurred, or perhaps, following Laing, one could speak of a breakthrough. In any case, as Luke's gospel puts it, "thoughts of many hearts stood revealed."

I have often been led to reflect that an immediate crisis, dumped incontinently into slavish routine, serves to clarify issues, hidden urges, ambitions, cowardice, fear—all of which previously have reposed in merciful obscurity. The obscurity is, of course, to the advantage of the interests involved. Indeed, on most campuses, there exists an Obscurity Machine. It churns away a perpetual twilight in which the gold of moral realities and questions of conscience are ground to chaff.

At Winnipeg, the crisis that laid bare our bones was a strike of maintenance workers. Peremptorily, one morning, without consulting the demands and appetites of our pampered nursery, some two thousand workers laid down brooms, towels, buckets, mops, and other assorted insignia of servitude. Immediately, the debris piled up, the toilets clogged; we, the darlings of the upper air, were in danger of drowning in our own garbage. And our servants and handmaids lined up, shivering in the icy weather, demanding (as I discovered by investigating matters at every available point) something so outrageous as a living wage.

Now it seemed to me that we had here something old-fashioned and simple; a religious issue. On the one hand, the president of the University, his subalterns and the faculties, were positively pneumatic with emoluments: conditions on Cloud Nine were never of higher advantage.

And the view of common earth from the heights? As I learned on many an occasion, it was comfortably remote, those on the heights could hardly take seriously the plight of families forced to live on one-fourth or one-fifth the median salary of the first estate.

Having learned such facts, what was one to do? I moved off campus. I explained to the students that if they wished to continue the classes, I could be discovered downtown, where friends among the Franciscans had offered me a room.

Thus, as things developed, we found ourselves, teacher and students, crossing another sort of line, crossing the absurd and tricky boundary that separates taught and teacher, marking off two fates where but one beckons; two orbits; collision and no community.

Found ourselves also at the side of the workers, affectively and actually. Enduring the picket line with them, bringing coffee and food, testing something of that fine purpose and grit that made working families embrace danger and insecurity, the price of achieving a status due to sentient and prideful beings. A lesson, need one add, of which the swaddled scions of oil, banking, landholding, and usury, stood in some need.

I also sought out my colleagues in the religion department, to discover what might be done in and out of classes, to raise the issue of the strike, and support our sisters and brothers, the working people of the University.

And met with the coldest shoulder ever raised in that arctic climate. Such matters as social injustice did not touch on their conception of religion. It was as simple as that, and as brutal. Indeed, if I read their eyes correctly, it was I who stood in need of instruction on the proper functioning of the department, which in no case was to be conceived as a threshing floor for the rude affairs of this world. . . .

There was the hilarious incident involving one renowned translator of the mysterious ways of God. His daily trek at mid-morning to the food bar to procure an apple was interrupted one day by a rather tentative group of students, requesting him to refuse to purchase food introduced on campus by scab arrangement. Our religious sibyl, sweeping aside the interfering helots in a hissing cloud of righteousness, procured and made off with his prey.

I later explained to friends, in the lingo endemic to high culture, that the guru was, in fact, and contrary to appearances, innocent of appetite. That he was, in fact, intent on reenacting the Fall for the benefit of all, especially those too unventuresome or airy of head to make the primordial leap into worldly knowledge. . . .

That year is long gone, and undoubtedly the religious department of the University of Manitoba is the better for my absence. But a minority report is sometimes useful, at least to a minority. And I hold to this day a bitter and vivid memory of the silence of "religious experts" when the rights of workers to bread and lodging and dignity were placed in question by a voracious consumer clan.

The event of the strike and its outcome, and the part played by myself and others, became for me a kind of luminous instant, a recognition scene; in it, like an awful public clockworks, each figure lurched in sight to play an appointed role in the dance of the death of the culture. A culture that rots first in its noblest parts. I had smelled the rot once more, and been nauseated by it, the proud ignorance of those whose narrow knowledge and narrower consciences bit to the bone.

Walking that morgue, where dead minds aped the ways of the living, I strengthened my resolve to live before I died.

5

In 1977, I went to live with the Buddhists in Paris. This was a community of Vietnamese exiles, declared personae non-gratae by Thieu and his successors during the worst of the war years. Some had been imprisoned, some died, a few made it out of Vietnam. My dearest friend in the community, the monk Thich Nhat Hanh, had been one of the Merton circle in the early '60s, when he lived and taught and traveled our country, denouncing the crimes of war and proposing, unequivocally and gently, the Buddhist alternative: stop the killing.

There was little simpatico for such a message. The American peace people were crying for the withdrawal of Americans from Vietnamese soil, or were defending the increasingly savage resistance of the Viet Cong and the North. Among Americans this Vietnamese monk stood, a solitary exotic, a man of silence and sublime naïveté, one of those figures whose innocence is an affront, who quite simply go their way amid a welter of the worldly wise, the traffickers, the opportunists and wise ones of this world (the contrariness of whom, and their hot and cold maunderings have also at times been my own).

That multipurpose apartment in suburban Paris; I see a small room in which I studied and meditated through the spring months of 1976. I was being healed. I was being healed of America, of the Western Church, of the Jesuits, of the wounds of war, of prison, of the disease of making it, of my race in time against time. I kept my old New York horarium, late nights of reading and prayer, late mornings, afternoon walks, study, evening conversations with Nhat Hanh. In the park of Sceaux, I sought out a remote corner and sat amid the flowering trees to consider my lot, my life, my foolish and steady heart, steady in the foolishness of peacemaking, determined in the manner of that organ to pursue its own beat.

Spring was abroad, springlike was the weather indoors, the weather of my moods. I walked as a stranger amid the chic crowds of the Paris suburb, I went my way as I had in New York and elsewhere. On clement days, to the park, home around sunset, a stop for brandy and coffee, the extravagant deluxe half-hour of the day. And, in the park, solitude and writing and reading.

In the evening we talked, after a short meditative silence, Nhat Hanh and I; talked slowly, like veterans whose scars and honors and dishonors and narrow squeaks could all be taken for once, for granted. Each looked in the other's eyes, and said what he saw there; and from there, in that refraction, what we saw of the world, of war, of community, of the horrors and glories of the past decade, of faith, of the deaths of those we loved. Those were good hours, part of the healing. Out of them, for my part, arose a new will which was a very old will, always in need of the strengthening of other lives; that we live, sensibly, modestly, the scope and valor of the gospel. Live it, so to speak, in corners, only half in sight; but with a stubborn jealousy, too, on my part, to be my own man, to possess my own soul. To make sense, first of all, and solidly, to myself, but with an admixture of craziness, too. Like a vein in stone, that at the shear, adds interest and beauty and draws the eye.

A third eye? It rested there in my forehead, like the savage primary eye in a peacock feather. I closed my two eyes, saw something prophetic and dark and beckoning. Saw precisely nothing, which is the truest vision of all, a *nada* that neither precedes creation nor depends from it. But within the world and time is something like a call, an obscure journey, a way unknown but possible. I look back on that road now, the road traversed since those months. It is no better illumined in memory than it was in prospect: still, it seems reasonably direct and morally unhedged. I walk by that vision, but I also walk with my feet.

◁ ○ ▷

Today, as hideous events all but whelm the consciences that never saw the flood rising, today I am rediscovered. I find myself dusted off, brought into public view. Something like the dusting off of a museum piece which the ebb of chic and taste has consigned to a storeroom, but which the recall of something long lost sight of (integrity of line, vehemence of vision, a finicky, persistent breakthrough?) clamors for once more. Something to offer, something to say!

The months in Sceaux, a rose tattoo in memory.

◁ ○ ▷

What the Buddha and Jesus and a few others talked about, commended, was, it seems to me, simply what they had seen.

No point in getting heavy about such matters. Visionaries, the genuine ones, don't live by vision anyway. What they insist on, and swear by (literally) is living. The conviction that life is its own orb and value and faithful amen.

6

I delivered, in 1974, a speech on Israel and the Palestinians. My words were ill-received by mainline intellectuals and church people, Jews and Christians. Some new epithets were coined for my improvement, some older ones dusted off, conferred anew, with considerable heat. I lost a number of friends, access to media, editors, magazines. Doors closed on their hinges, and were not again opened.

A few years later, at a New England meeting of the Catholic Peace Fellowship, I attempted to draw certain analogies, connections, between vexed moral questions.

I summoned my hapless chutzpah once more; to suggest that in Pentagon and abortion mill there existed moral squalor and darkness, a common will to settle human difficulties in the way of the quack; namely by disposing of humans themselves.

Again, I was ill-received, this time by a large group of women, many of them Catholics, many of them wounded mothers of aborted children.

Amid such toil and trouble, there is no point in trying to concoct a "good speech," whatever that might mean. One might dream of words which were mollifying to all parties, and at the same time, morally truthful. Impossible: we are beginners in drawing such connections as I attempted; so I speak clumsily, and wound many. But perhaps one can claim, in soul's privacy, the coldest comfort of all. That I have tried to the best of ability and study to bring a measure of light to bear on dark and neglected corners of existence.

I have not been able to persuade myself that on those occasions I worked permanent harm. Quite the contrary. After the Israeli-Palestinian speech there fell, with speed, vitriol, discernment, and much folly, a very Niagara of responses. And along with other developments that could not have been foreseen, there occurred a striking change of moral atmosphere. For the first time since the foundation of Israel, the Palestinian people began to appear on the retina of America's eye. Very nearly vanished before! What a horrifying near victory that was, that a whole people, inhabiting the world, should all but disappear from sight, like a purgatorial ghost at dawn!

But they were not ghosts; they were less insubstantial than we, morally speaking. They showed themselves to the world, a people of flesh and blood, by bleeding, by letting blood. But we would not see. And when I insisted on their rights—insisted there would be no peace while their rights were trampled under—it was as though the messenger must be killed for his bad news.

The days immediately following such episodes were a shambles. It is a terrible thing to be called publicly an anti-Semite; not just by opportunists and camp followers (this could be borne with), but by friends of long standing. It is almost equally terrible, a new defamation, to be named a hater of women. It goes against the grain of the soul, it is a brutish knife laid against a living tissue. With intent to kill? Certainly to do harm, to hurt, to force silence, to declare taboos.

◁ ○ ▷

Such events can be taken lightly only by those who have not felt their pain. To say I felt their pain, and carry the pain to this day, is simply the truth.

Death itself I consider a lesser pain than estrangement. Pain not only to myself, but to my friend as well. A double suffering, each separately inflicted, insupportable, moreover, to the degree that the friendship was of long duration, apparently well-founded, a mutuality the years had tested and proved sound.

But not sound enough. Not under such crisis.

◁ ○ ▷

There is yet another aspect to such loss. I have a sense that the times themselves, apart from more or less deliberately created crises, render strong things fragile, and fragile things mortally endangered. The times themselves are a permanent crisis.

It is as though the egg of the universe were attacked by an environment gone mad. The embryo infected, the shell thinned, unable to carry its burden of life to term. In such a situation, what heel would fall wantonly on the endangered nest?

And how describe or indeed, understand, such double jeopardy? or guard against it?

◁ ○ ▷

Perhaps one like myself is no more than an exotic, a primitive, a survivor in a loincloth among the civilized, a sport washed up by tides.

One either clothes himself and learns good manners, or is made to disappear. The choices are not wide.

Let me think for a moment of these "civilized," of whom I am one. I belong to the second generation after the one described by Bonhoeffer as "come of age." In this hypothesis, technology and mastery of the forces of nature have nudged us forward, given us, so to speak, the final genetic kick out of social adolescence. Now we are the masters of worlds within, of a universe humanized beyond the wildest primitive dream.

Come of age! To be sure, certain elements of the theory are still lacking. There is a malaise in the air, things are going ill for many, afflicted with poverty, disease, early death, lifelong misery. There exists, even among the fortunate, a kind of free-floating anxiety, an outlook that has its own peculiar "inlook," a lack of breadth, of generosity, a sense of life damaged, of structures that disserve. . . .

◁ ○ ▷

Meantime, with a vision of my own, and with my friends, and step by step, and without encouragement and guidance, I went on repeating, in many tongues and symbolic acts, a simple and central command: "Thou shall not kill."

Thou shalt not kill? But who disagreed? Surely not the decent Christians, the "people of God," the scientists, the professionals, the Niebuhrians, the apolitical intellectuals, those who serve their country in Pentagon and think tank and laboratory, those whose "high security clearance" defines their Christianity also.

Christianity as "also." It may be our obituary.

◁ ○ ▷

1975. A friend and I discussed whether a trip to the Near East might be of import. Our conclusion was that a visit to Israel was indeed in order; but that the trek ought to include a crossing into Arab countries; Egypt, Syria, Lebanon. And finally, a return to Israel to report on our findings.

Considerable difficulties had to be dealt with. At that time, no one could enter Israel whose passport showed a prior visit to Arab countries. Our plan therefore was to reenter Israel through Cyprus, the Arab countries being amenable to having visits left unrecorded on our documents.

So it was done.

I dwell on this trip because it is intimately related to beliefs already set down here; the connections that I believe hold between violence and deception.

Let me illustrate. In Lebanon and Syria we undertook exchanges with Palestinian leaders, Arafat, Hawatma, and George Habash. We made plain our intent, that we came among them to learn first-hand the plight of the Palestinian people; that we wished at the same time, to express certain convictions, forged in the fires of anti-war resistance in the United States. We represented no church, or government, nor were we journalists, out for a scoop.

We were received with courtesy and more.

I saw that in this instance, as in others, the great world of tumultuous rhythms welcomes such specimens as ourselves, whose moral and political choices rest on bases far different than those commonly in vogue. And at the same time, a hint comes through—of something forgotten, something neglected or violated in the soul. There was admiration in the eyes of these bold men of iron; we were strangers indeed, but we could not be accounted enemies. Nor had we come such great distance, at such trouble, in order to furbish our ego or "prove a point."

What then were they to make of us? From Vietnam to these guarded camouflaged rooms which we entered under the guns, was a short step indeed. Nor were guns a strange or shocking sight to us. We had seen guns before, indeed, they were an international phenomenon; every nation state was a gunrunner, ours number one. To us, the guns were more in the nature of a boring stereotype, the least impressive cliché of history. They spoke of a mirage of expectations forever receding, a revolution perpetually invoked, incanted, paid its tribute of blood—and never arriving. Indeed, if their salvo announced anything, it was the opening of the ghost dance of the "new man."

New? human? We held other expectations, other visions and voices pressed on us. These gentlemen, severally clothed in khaki, in mufti, in a business suit (the clothing seeming to stand for a kind of personal timetable; from hope deferred, to victory all but grasped)—they spoke, if they could but hear one another (and they could not, being sorely at odds), spoke a tongue so common as to be synchronized with the tongues of the makers and breakers of humanity; and I write this in a sense that pays no compliment to their purported understanding, either of true history or of the hopes of humanity.

I mean that one among them deceived us: I believe the deceit was committed in full deliberation. Further, that deception, far from being startling or exceptional is, in fact, the common method of violent intent and act.

The deceit was either overt or implied, but it was there.

In the first instance, we were assured by Hawatmah that his organization had abandoned terrorism as a tactic some years before. His assurances were so startlingly like those of the founder of the Irish Provos! No more violence, no more strafing of airports, no more murder of athletes, no more nicely calculated assassinations on foreign soil. What had occurred was done with. Or so we were assured.

The assurances were a lie. And whether Paul and I were to be accounted mere innocents abroad, jackrabbits in a snake pit, seems to me to miss the point. We believed the gentleman, or we wanted to believe him—which perhaps comes to the same thing. We wanted to believe that a movement with an overwhelming weight of justice on its side, with world opinion raging on its behalf—that world all but ready at long last, to take seriously the violated rights of the Palestinians—that such a movement could abandon its earlier frenzies, cast off its murderous memories. We wanted to believe that commandos and those who commanded them could grow up—into humans. We believed moreover, that apart from the illegitimate character of murder, a simple sense of tactics would argue that in Israel-Palestine, murder was gettting nowhere.

So we took comfort in the disclaimer, and hoped for the best. Only to discover some weeks later, on our return to Israel, that Commander Hawatmah's commandos were once again on the prowl in Israel. This time they had seized a schoolhouse in Galilee, with the usual outcome: the deaths of children, the deaths of soldiers. Our revulsion and anger can perhaps be imagined. There was the question of murder, there was the question of deceit: a deceit wrought by those who had posed as our friends. So we prepared a statement that quoted the disclaimers of Hawatmah, and went on the radio in Tel Aviv to tell the story of the Lebanon meeting, of the assurances so speedily and bloodily violated.

It is painful beyond words to recall such events; bringing them up once more seems to push the sane world out of joint.

We felt betrayed; there are, I submit, few worse blows to be endured. But the pain of the blow cannot be described as simply the impact of a fist against one's body. The betrayer was indeed betraying Paul and me, and that was damage enough. But he was also betraying his own people, whose cause was tainted by yet one more crime. He was inviting reprisal upon the innocent and aged and ill, the children of the terrifying camps of southern Lebanon; reprisals that continue to this day, prompt and terrible.

Moreover, he was clouding the Palestinian issue before the world, making it easier for the "enemy" to justify, in turn, the murder of Palestinian children, a child's eye for a child's eye, a milk tooth for a milk tooth, the *lex talionis* turned against innocents. Can one conceive of a greater horror, the children first as hostages, then as victims of such hatred!

One saw in a nightmare Dame Justice shudder where she stood; one saw her necessary blindness turned to partial sight, scales thrown off balance. For after such crimes against Israeli children, Israel, whose cause stood suspect before the world, was supplied with a cause by those least apt to lend her one. They had betrayed themselves, they had given Israel child martyrs.

Let me speak also of what I take to be a continuing and covert betrayal by such leaders. They stand in the very breach of history; and they are helpless to read the signs of the times. They know nothing of new ways—toward a coherent society, dignity, a rightful place in the world—new ways that are also very old ways. Before ever they win their national state, they are locked in the old discredited methods of the national state. They want armies and guns, a plethora of guns, the latest guns; and more—diplomacy and Grand Hotels and Mercedes-Benzes and a defense budget and police and prisons. They want a social structure that, elsewhere, stands dead in its boots. They want, if it were possible, that ultimate credit card, membership in the nuclear club, which might more properly be called the International Suicide Club. They want alignments and blocs; and whether they voice such appetites standing in fatigues or diplomats' silks, seems to me beside the point. Which is perhaps a point already sufficiently belabored, or perhaps not. But which is meant to be a cry on behalf of all those, children and women and the aged, the ill, and poor who perish in the camps of southern Lebanon each day, or who in smaller numbers die in Israel.

But always, it must be insisted, someone dies. And invariably, those who die have no vote in whether they live or die. And invariably, those who bear responsibility in such matters do not themselves die. They live on, to decree the deaths of others.

What will come of this trade-off and write-off of victims, what political forms will emerge, remains obscure. Still I will venture a prediction: very little new will come of it, yet another nation state will arise, its first generation presided over by those who once pushed illegitimate terror (all pre-state terror being illegitimate) and now push legitimate terror (the legitimate terror named war). The citizens of the new state will be those, many or few, who have survived the fiery years in the camps, the children who learned the manual of arms as their first alphabet, and held a real, not an imaginary gun, as their first toy. The idealist warriors will become realists, statesmen. The ideologues will turn homeward at last; the historians, the scholars of every discipline, the religious leaders, to be tolerated in the new regime in proportion to their approval of the terror that preceded its existence, the violence that is to follow.

The new state, beside the hardly older state; our fervent hope, if we are lucky. And soon may it come to be; the sooner the luckier, in view of the nuclear weapons of Israel and of South Africa, her ally.

Granted even this singular luck, a peaceable outcome of the contemporary Middle East horrors, the hypothetical outcome will be a time of waiting and watching and hoping; and also of skepticism and a sinking heart, based on the outcome of every violent revolution of our lifetime. Can peace and humanity and internal justice issue from consistent injustice, murder, the blunting of minds toward innocent life? The questions touch and afflict both sides, if perchance they grow thoughtful.

7

There was the episode of the Hibernian Heroes.

I had been invited to Ireland to offer a retreat at Glencree, a

Reconciliation Center in the Wicklow Mountains outside
Dublin. It was a raucous five or six days; from the North came
Protestants and priests, from all over came feminists,
supporters of the IRA, a few Jesuits, students, teachers. The
air was so hot with contention that by the third day, a
suggestion seemed imperative. That we retire for a day from
the business at hand and make our separate ways into the hills
nearby, to take counsel with ourselves, and perhaps allow a
more peaceable spirit to speak.

It turned out well. That evening, we offered the cooks and
scullions a dinner prepared by ourselves instead of them.
There followed music and dancing and hilarity, and by next
morning, we were prepared for a different rhythm.

At the close of our retreat, it was proposed that the people of
Dublin be invited to our center for a general meeting, to be
addressed by me. I concurred, and on the following Sunday, a
considerable crowd assembled.

After the main proceedings, I was approached by a rather
taciturn man, inquiring as to my interest in sitting for a while
with a few friends of the Irish resistance. His words were
sufficiently veiled to convey an impression that something
unusual was in the air. I agreed, and a group rather quickly
came together in a remote room of the house.

Three members of the Provisional wing of the IRA had been
in the audience, and were now seated before me. They
included the founder of the Provos, a large, florid man
recently released from a long prison sentence. There was also a
priest whose function seemed to be to preside at the funerals of
IRA warriors summarily removed from this world. The third
refused to identify himself; I had the impression he was on the
run.

What ensued was, as I recall, a heated and ragged exchange
around topics like violence, nonviolence, piety, denials of
complicity, settings right of the record, denunciations of the
British, affirmations of loyalty to the church; a curious Irish
stew of every ingredient and savor and surprise; from prime

beef to Missus Murphy's overalls. It was ludicrous and tragic, it was music hall and street bloodshed, it summoned the rambunctious ghosts of Parnell and O'Connell and the dead of the Easter uprising, without forgetting the Blessed Virgin Mary and our holy father the Pope. And the rosary. And the bombs. Which may God be our judge, it isn't our people who t'row, but the British, who as long as they occupy our fair land, every Irish lad will be in arms, so help me God.

The priest was mum, the third man glum; all this asseverating and negating and swearing by Bibles and beads was done by our friend the founder, the ex-con. He sat there in the little box of a room, the rest of us silent for the main part; there were memories and fears and a trail of blood across the floor. And the lenghtening shadows of a mountain day, that color and tone of nature, so perfect and so doomed, the long setting to the short and sharp light, the summer of Ireland. We huddled there, he chain-smoked with his nervous chubby hands, his suit shapeless as a sack, he overweight, foolish, nondescript, yet crowned with the indefensible dignity of the prisoner, the prisoner of conscience—the dignity of even the wrong conscience.

I was appalled, and I loved him. Our eyes met, we knew something. We stood in the same leaky boat, the botched curragh of the world, opposite numbers, the transplanted Irish and the rooted. Each with a taste of jail in his mouth, the look, hangdog and stubborn, of the ex-prisoner. He calling the shots, and I deflecting them.

For he denied it all. They had given up on bombing, the Provos, as God was his judge. It was the bloody British, planting such things in such places as would implicate the Provisionals. Making it seem, God curse them, as though the Irish were the guilty party, north or south.

He renounced violence, he said. And yet he hedged curiously about the question of nonviolence. What was their method anyway, what was the tactic? He was fingering his rosary by now; just as a priest was part of the paraphernalia of terror, so now was the Blessed Virgin. And in the presence of these two numina, the Virgin and the celibate warrior, the one to bury the dead, the other to raise them to paradise—in light of these two, the events of this world were small potatoes, indeed. Bombs, bullets, strikes, sabotage, votes, constituencies, Catholics, Protestants, gun-running, the corpse in the alley, the long somber procession to the grave, the volleys skyward, the black box sinking, the indomitable women—it was death for portion and tithe and prospect. The British be damned, on with the wars of the just!

They told me off (a while later they would tell the Pope off). Ireland, dead or alive, was their business, not mine.

I learned a few things that afternoon which I had learned elsewhere, and which were assuming a shape in my mind, the shape of a truism. Learning this; that as surely as the hand takes up a bomb or a gun, the mind takes up a lie.

That the two are parts of a single tactic, call it terror or violence. In order to kill and call the killing politics, you must justify the killing. And the best way to justify killing is to deny that one kills at all. The hand signs the death warrant, the mind rips it up, denies it exists. And someone dies—always, inevitably, the children, the old, the defenseless.

This is the diplomacy of hedgerow and ditch. It is also a sign, among other things, that yet another nation state is being incubated. The lies put together by a few anonymous iron-faced men in a darkened room, in a remote barn loft, in an alley—as the resistance movement swells, as skirmishes are won, as the knot of fighters weaves and advances and comes closer to the day of victory; as the future takes shape, the lies and deception and charges and counter-charges, what we might call the raw ideology of the commando—this will shortly be replaced by an alphabet of the elite, the nuances and feints of international intrigue, CIA's, KCIA's, SAVAK's, the diplomat's stripes, cigars, brandies, the rascal look, the scoundrel pressing the flesh, power, police, emoluments, pride of place.

Let these reflections convey no mere cynicism. From prison to hedgerow to palace, is I believe, by no means the necessary course of revolution, its degradation is by no means inevitable. But such a degradation remains highly likely, as experience shows so bitterly. And the defeat of noble intent grows more likely when guns have been the instruments of overthrow.

The guns, as I have suggested elsewhere, have an altogether uncanny tendency to take over. Eventually they rule the gunmen. One kills, after a while, with a high and even euphoric detachment. As though when a body thuds to earth, and the smoking gun is lowered once more, one sees with elation a cleared space, an obstacle removed. A mirage, no doubt, a utopia, but how seductive! The gunman breathes easier, salvation is at hand.

I recently saw a poster in the office of a minister of religion, a collage of photos of a Latin priest, Camilo Torres, one photo imposed on another, from light hue to dark. In the first image, the priest is attired in a soutane, in the second in a business suit, in the third in commando fatigues, a submachine gun in his embrace.

The image stopped my heart. It gathered in one the nearly unbearable ironies of my life.

To those who composed the image (and to the one who displayed it) the poster undoubtedly celebrates a passage from a lower to a higher order of vocation. More eloquently than words, it spoke of the passage of a priest from his demeaning and bizarre costume, into a "real" world, that world where the gun speaks loud and clear, the gun whence power issues in flames.

For me, the design meant something utterly different; a derangement, a sign of crazy times. Priests as gunmen.

There is a symbol of considerable moment here, if only we have the wit to grasp it. Let me call it the "homogenesis of hell." For in hell, are not all alike? And could not this likeness be construed as the ultimate genetic development, a development denied us here on earth?

Let us earthlings announce the triumph, in anticipation. In hell, let every creature possess a gun. With this altogether breathtaking difference, that the damned do not buy, sell, tote their guns; they grow them, a logical and literal second nature.

Alas, we are not yet in hell: in our vale of tears, the gun-toting priests offer little succor in our plight. . . .

Let it only be said that when priests brandish guns, it is by no means surprising that other gun-wielders, whether nuclear or "conventional," feel their muscle double in might; since (to revert to our poster, and the mind that conceived it) the gun (nuclear or conventional) clearly as of now has a blessing laid on it.

And let it be *dignum et justum,* a source of consolation to the dead (as well as to those who love and mourn them) that they perished under a blessed bullet.

A blessing of Mars, god of guns? words fail.

8

I bring up the following with a sense of unease, discomfiture. My life is, as I am often informed, disruptive.

Do I not, in effect, roll an apple of discord down the long liturgical table, where a sophisticated rite is in progress?

Call this a phantasy; it is in fact, something real, surreal. A Christian liturgy gets underway, the guitars tune up, the hymns are raised. And I see something else. Not the light-hearted, easy-going worship of campus and parish. A secular liturgy in progress across the world; another sort of banquet than that of Christians.

Are we ignorant of this other proceeding? If we are, our own is something other than we imagine it; a feast of fools.

That other banquet is as scripturally verifiable as the Eucharist itself. It is described in chapter 19, verse 17 of Revelation. Trestles, we are told, have been set up at intervals across the world. Atop these, bare boards are arranged.

And what takes place then, beggars description—even our

own, who have supped on a lifetime of horror. A cannibal feast is in progress. It is a nightmare, it is an image of our world, an anti-Eucharist.

◁ ○ ▷

There are a sublime few whom I count mentors through their writings, one or two of them Jesuits, their works recently discovered once more. As I listen again to their voices, they seem to me lacking in one crucial area. It is as though they had lighted my path at every point except one—the point where my path ended at a precipice. At the verge, their light was quenched. And I must grope to the edge alone, or go over the edge. But there they can neither warn nor lead.

Is this the human circumstance; or is it merely my own bad luck, that I have not found, among the classical minds and their resonant and winning truthfulness, any help at that edge; an edge which is mathematical, verifiable, and yet beyond fathoming?

At that point, my only guide is one who has gone further, who has fallen in, who has died. And is, in principle, unable to tell me where the path ended, where and how he fell. Or what lies at the bottom of the chasm. But he tells me nonetheless—by having done these things, endured them. And I will know more—only at the bottom.

◁ ○ ▷

The temptation to "give up" on others invariably comes to rest, like a buzzard on living meat, on those closest to me; close by vow, by long friendship. But the thing is always subtle, the horrid interest of the buzzard eye is not in buzzard meat. Who are the Jesuits to me anyway? They answer the question in a thousand half perceptible ways, year upon year.

(But this is coping badly with the question, which was first raised by me, and not them, at least on this page.)

A continuing scandal, a blank wall, a seedy inventory; cowardice and evasion and self-indulgence and hankering after this world. . . . All this wells up in me. And then betimes a better spirit prevails. It whispers: Don't forget, you're also talking about yourself.

And still I am not talking about myself, I am talking about another world, another version of reality, other voices, other rooms than those I inhabit.

As we Jesuits were once the tightest little island in the universe, and would speedily offer a ferry ticket to the mainland to any of our number who had "difficulties with obedience," so now we suffer the most grievous incursions of any order. The tightest spring explodes first.

What we are left with, after all the rococo rhetoric, is a rather loose federation of nation-state individuals, privately virtuous (to a point), publicly courteous to one another (invariably, the officers' club rules). Existence lightened here and there and now and then, by friendships that crack the code.

And in a deadly sort of way, efficient, smooth to the touch.

And toward the end of life, stoic and lonely and set of face toward death.

And receiving into the company of purpose and fore-thought, the youth—created to our image and likeness, which is to say, old before they are young.

And here and there, unpredictably, cast up on shore, biological sports of faithful understanding, a hero or two in every generation, Judas goats to expiate the indolence, indifference, academic, entrepreneurial mind of the tribe.

And casting up an equal number of charlatans and Judases who make the goats and their bloody demise anthropologically necessary. For every fascist Shah, Nixon, Marcos, etc., an S.J. to bless the bloody proceedings. You know it.

The official line, meantime, being something to redden the ear of an angel. Self-congratulation, stern admonition, drawing of lines, catenation of thunders. And what machismo!

Also money, money, money. And buildings. A pathetic aping of the gargantuan appetite of the state and the consumers of academe. Making it in the world, a religious enterprise. Uriah Heep smacking lips as the clichés roll out:

What's wrong with institutional well-being? Behold, how the Lord blesses his own! And what's your problem?

Learning, in harness to moral inertia. The distinctions that paralyze; for every authority another authority, for every "on the one hand," an "on the other." The rhetoric that kills.

And then, and then, the gleam of devotion, the lifelong work and struggle in hidden places. The ego contained and sweetened by prayer and obscure suffering. The heroes, the fools, the breakthroughs, the untouchable and incorruptible, the work horses, the scholars, the sweetness and strength of those who serve, the remnant that saves the whole bloody adulterated mess.

Perhaps our present plight is also a kind of salvation. At last, the "two worlds," one of privilege and connivance and sucking up to the rich, the other, the hero without mother country or tongue—these two are at last out in the light, we know our degraded and self-humiliated state, we know that we despise and fear women and homosexuals, that we tolerate, indeed cultivate, a first and second and third estate of citizenship, of works and pomps.

One has to dig deeper than the sixteenth century to resurrect the Christ in the baroque tomb.

9

When we discussed, in a class of the urban poor in South Bronx, what Martin King and Malcolm X meant to their people, one invariable answer was offered. "They didn't give us up. They didn't betray us."

I thought that would not be a bad *sigillum,* a seal on the soul: He didn't betray. It had overtones and resonances, all across board and bed, whether in marriage or friendship or politics or the church. "Not to betray" might almost be a translation of that other primitive command that governs my life and thought: not to kill. Maybe it is all one.

◁ ○ ▷

Please bear with a contrast to the above. I was invited to pass a day at a prestigious engineers' school, a place of icy competence and moral dereliction, where the old induct the young into the mysteries of nuclear extinction.

After a sleepless night (my vigil encouraged by the drunken caterwauling of graduate students), I was required to appear at a luncheon, and face questioning. I ventured to prime the pump by declaring my misgivings about arrangements whereby sciences are put in service to the nuclear warmaking state. The pump promptly yielded a flood, indignant questioning as to my daring to place limits on the "value-free research of the university. . . . !"

The shibboleth had taken hold. My patience fled me; in any case, I had a bus to catch.

"Let me only say," I replied mildly, "my strongest objection is that you are planning my murder."

And departed, without great regret on either side.

◁ ○ ▷

In December of 1980, I was invited to Berkeley for a semester at the Jesuit seminary there. I sit here on the Berkeley hillside like a cricket on its haunches, singing dismay at a somnolent hearth. Everything is—not so much "normal" (who wants normalcy in Berkeley?), but chic, hyped, mellow—from theology to street hustling. On our hill, the air is positively blue with supernatural essence, the pure opposite of pollution: God talk perhaps. Tolerant folk, well-heeled, well-dressed, the latest evanescent absurdity, hip language, a compound of psychobabble and street smarts.

Nonetheless, there is a generous and sweet feeling in the air, the free clinic panhandles and makes it, the disabled move along with the able-bodied, I seem worlds away from the despair, anomie, morose spirit of New York. Something here sheathes the knife edge of survival, the horrifying sense that one survives on the shoulders of others' drowning.

Let me not discount what I see, or glorify East Coast cynicism.

And yet, and yet, what is easily enjoyed is often cheaply won. In the pinched blue faces of the New York subway, in the mad mumbling freezing bag ladies, in the conundrums, slush, speed, distraction—do I not have there also a genuine rhythm, a testing, something of survival hardily won, something truer and closer to the bone of the times?

◁ ○ ▷

At the edge of my community, I meet those at the edge of other communities. This is a bitter advantage I was first led to ponder by Merton. And I vowed I will never make a virtue of alienation. But on the other hand, I will not consent to disappear into America.

◁ ○ ▷

They have a master of liturgy here, an expert of note, committees that plan and coordinate and I don't know what. And yet it all manages by a kind of perverse wonder, to be stiff-necked and weightless and superficial, like a well-choreographed, badly written slice of show biz. Or like a blind man, taking soundings of the air and concluding that all is made of air. Meantime, forgetting that his feet rest against something other than air.

What do our feet rest against, what do our hands grasp? It might be good to begin liturgy with such questions.

◁ ○ ▷

One Jesuit friend has done me the honor of attending my course. He is a scholar of note, no sycophant.

He reports that he finds me obsessed with death. More, that little or nothing comes through my classes (though he gives reluctant assent to my analysis of events)—about "building the kingdom, doing our part, here and now, to create a future."

Now, I had fondly thought that such "building," apart from self-testing, resistance, legal jeopardy, was a great illusion, one tending to no good outcome. Tending rather to obfuscation, moral bewilderment. But in no sense, or only in a grudging minimal sense, meeting the realities of the times. Which I take to be, simply, the proliferating and legitimizing of murder as simple social method.

But such reflections among Jesuits, young and old, are commonly taken as fanatical or worse, and best steered away from.

◁ o ▷

While I was teaching in Berkeley, my friend Tony Towne died suddenly on Block Island. He and Bill Stringfellow had "harbored" me in '70 when the FBI were hot on my heels; in fact, it was from their home that I was flushed, a harmless faun indeed. To be hustled off a durance vile. During the months that followed, the conduct of these two friends was exemplary, as one would have expected. Their indictment but whetted the sword of the spirit, their jeopardy grown sharp as our own. And finally, what a relief, the government dropped charges against them, as being publicly indefensible.

But the friendship never wavered. It was like a baptism, conferred rather than deserved, and conferred but once in a lifetime.

Tony was a great bear of a man, with a heart that exceeded its space. He was a solitary, the island was his hermit's cave. From its mouth, he observed, with elegant wit and disciplined detachment, the worsening of our lot. It was due to him that, among other benefits more personal to myself, many of us found in the Island a few "undeveloped" acres of sanity and peace, and thither repaired on occasion.

◁ o ▷

We have at the seminary large numbers of students, Protestant and Catholic. Many of them, I discover, are trying to become something other than simply Protestant and/or Catholic. Maybe they are trying to be Jewish? That, granted (1) the present state of Protestants and Catholics, and (2) the place both Protestant and Catholics come from—that may not be a bad idea.

◁ o ▷

I wanted to discover something both specific and maddeningly difficult by teaching at the Berkeley seminary. Something like this: what was happening under what was happening. This might even be called a religious project. Then it suddenly occurred to me one day, I think in reading something of Charles Olson—this was exactly what I had been trying to do in Revelation class, to reach, not the phenomena, nor the noumena either, for in neither lay the true and absorbing interest of scripture.

There was a clue in Revelation 11, the fate of the "two witnesses." Almost exactly halfway through the passage, the tense abruptly changes, from future to past. A strange reversal of worldly expectation, of our all but innate conviction that worldly ways bring something referred to as "progress."

None of this. Everything that "happened" in the lives and deaths of the two witnesses, as the empire icily regarded their work and brought about their deaths, is placed in the future tense, "not yet," but nonetheless certain. (And this, although at the time of writing such a fate as theirs would be by no means unusual or beyond predicting.) This, in effect, is how it will go with believers in the "real" world of power politics and capital justice. You (will inevitably) get put to death, your bodies (will) rot in the streets, Pilate and Herod (will) positively shudder with glee, the mobs (will) hold holiday.

Such a "future" the empire has in mind for those who disturb its false peace: a future at once inexorable, immaculately legal.

Thus a comment is offered, by way of parable, on the life and death of Christ. First, all this *will be* inflicted on you. Then, afterward, Something else *has happened;* something of a different order entirely, something so utterly certain, so explosive, that it can be clinched in past tense. Whereas the world's iron-bound murderous disposal of your life is put in the abominable future.

I thought some new sense of things, corresponding maybe to the difference between good news and bad, might be in question here. What if the essential good news were always considered as past, while the bad news of the world were thought of as future?

The first would express the certainty of faith and hope; which is to say, the really faithful and hopeful acts are everywhere and always already done, and done with. They are the truest stuff of true memory, they set us on fire because they have the absolute validity of fact, accomplishment.

And what if, always clouding the sun, always threatening and rattling away and muttering overhead (but never quite coming down, never quite making it, never having that final word, final solution, never quite the "mission accomplished" of death's power), stood the never entirely impeding and inhibiting bad decrees, threats, ill will, hatreds, fears, capital punishments, passings of bucks, making of wars—all, in fact, that we have seen in our lifetime, all we dread and cower under?

What if the claim of death to speak the last word concerning our fate—what if this word were never uttered? And this, even though the claim awakens such fear in us, such a hollow echo in the bones, that in effect it displaces the past, our true past, accomplished past—and routs that past, and makes of our hearts and heads a stable of the beast?

When the just die by inflicted violence, it is always in the future; that is the flat word of scripture. Learn history in this way. Which is to say, the just never allow that punishment to attain, in their understanding, the status of a sacred event, inevitable. The state can only threaten death, because to its worst (the "first death"; John) there corresponds a "second life."

This is by no means to deny that the state has a "worst" in its arsenal. We know by God that it has, and worse than worst. What we also know, in light of the biblical war of tenses, is that the worst is not bad enough to seize the position of the sacred past, the *opus operatum* in Christ. It can never seize us as the sacred seizes us.

This brings a new field of vision, especially in our attitude toward death. A question like, "who owns us anyway?"

I consulted the experts on all this, to discover if the change of tenses might mean what I suggest. But found little or nothing, one way or another.

Nor is the command to "measure the temple" taken as a clue (Rev. 11) that times of crises call for clear lines. In phony times of "normalcy" we drift along toward some murky Point Omega; everybody can come along, the ride is free. But then the skies fall in. And suddenly we want to know where we are, and with whom. So we "measure the temple," and by implication, we take our own measure as well. As Gandhi would say, we need a scripture to measure life by. And scripture advises also, measure your scripture, measure your temple; where your treasure is, there also is your heart.

◁ ○ ▷

Religious academics come up with distinctions like "prophetic" vs. "pastoral," and the young fry shoot the words off at you as though they came hot from Jesus. Thus do we turn our prophetic souls off and on, like Hal the computer, who has two speeds, slow forward and fast backward. Us, too.

◁ ○ ▷

Paul Goodman says there is no good education except growing up into a worthwhile world. One could also say, there is no good seminary except one grows up into a worthwhile church. The supposition of the bureaucrats and academics, peddled straight-faced, is that there is a worthwhile church to grow up into. This must be accounted one of the more ludicrous fictions of the age.

◁ ○ ▷

Of course there exists a worthwhile church; from my view, the expression is tautological. But its meaning and method are worlds apart from the "models" commonly proposed by mainliners.

What the young need, instead of hair splitting, abstraction, huffing and puffing liturgies, and secular folderol, is the taste of a worthwhile church. This, together with the skill and will to draw such a community together out of the ragtag and dog-eared and wounded and energetic and disillusioned. I note, meantime, without becoming romantic, that the best of the seminarians already have the look of the above, and the improvising skills required. What the best of them need is moral support and noninterference.

Meantime 90 percent of seminary "problems" arise from the suspicion which invades the dreams even of the chic and skilled. The suspicion is that things are going to pot; that we don't have much of a church to offer anyone, including ourselves.

◁ ○ ▷

It makes to smile, as the French say; quixotically, most good feeling about life today arises not from the swinish affluence of the sub- or urban desert, but from a common understanding of our plight, and doing something about it.

All sorts of heavy bombarding questions keep hitting such actions as are responsibly, civilly disobedient. Let the questions come, let things get clear. What ought to be a satisfaction is the joy, so humanly touching, that geysers up after such acts; the relief, the sense of something done, and well done, the animal spirits released, the dancing and partying and drinking and good food. Primary emotions let go that otherwise, neglected and unused, dry up in the soul. Tears unshed, laughter unspent—what a tragedy and diminishment to dwell forever on sere middle ground, landlocked.

◁ ○ ▷

This was the best day in a long time around the seminary, in the estimation of many (of me, too). Ash Wednesday, 1980. We had decided to urge Christians out of the theological sepulchre, where (to mix metaphors) they grew enchanted with images on cave walls.

The issue was an urgent one, the complicity of the U. of California in the notorious Livermore Labs, where every nuclear weapon in our land is concocted. The seminaries can be held complicit in these crimes in preparation, since we grant graduate degrees through the University. There exists, therefore, a kind of contemptible mutuality between the puffed secular on the one hand, and the sacred on the make. We glow in the sound of the carillons, they have God on their side.

No longer. Ash Wednesday, spartan, teach-in, workshops, solid education, stopping the show. Silence and liturgy and fasting. Then a procession to the university, mime, song, banners, the classic paraphernalia of conscience on the long march.

And, of course, a sit-in.

That "of course" indicates to me a noble habitude which evokes deep gratitude and admiration, the taking for granted of solid virtue in practice, a release from the lounging state-fed and -boarded consciences of university wards.

We sat in, a wide variety of our species. McAfee Brown, with that chin like a prow cutting through polluted and troubled waters; the Ellsbergs; Dan, like an electric eel; Patricia, gentle and contained and delighted to be in busted company at last; Louie the Franciscan provincial, a string bean of a man as native to the scene as a bean on a vine. (Will we ever have a Jesuit provincial so moved by events that he will refuse to "move on command"? That, given the stuck conscience of the Number One Order of Men *[sic]*, would indeed be the trumpet call of the kingdom!)

In that stuffy outer office of the University president they let us cool our posteriors for some nine hours, uncertain how to stifle the bell and quench the candle. That gave us time, needed time as things turned out, to reflect, pray, spread ashes, affix pictures of bombs to their walls, fast and sing and be silent by turn. Time enough and world, as the poet has it. And then, about midnight, they decided to "clear the property." We were rounded up, bug-eyed and elated, and printed and booked and ejected from the building. And there in the rain stood that rain-sodden crowd of friends, Romans, countrymen, come to bury Caesar and praise us. Hooting sax horn wove arpeggios and groans around our defiance, there were food and drink and hugs galore. As they used to say in the old manuals, most humans must taste purgatory before they can enjoy the Vision. Exactly.

In the course of our sit-in, one of the office subalterns screamed, "And you call yourselves religious people, coming in here under the shroud of God. . . ." This immediately after we had poured ashes on the floor. Meantime, up the hill, at one of the laboratories, I am told that the bomb concocters are also preparing to "carbon test" the Shroud of Turin. Is the shroud of God for real? Will we know at last?

We may know yet, in a far different way than anticipated, and the shroud of God may be vast enough to stretch across the corpse of all humanity.

◁ ○ ▷

I have a strange sense, in Berkeley, in March of 1980, that a forgotten history is coming alive before my eyes. Something that in other times and climes would appear merely as logic, good sense, Christian rightness, a sane response to crime; in such times as ours, it takes on the heady quality of the unheard of, the utterly and sumptuously overflowing spirit. One had not seen this in so long, one had grown used to crawling the earth like Kafka's metamorphosed bug, a cockroach with the soul of a human, the moral sense of a human, condemned to a cruel parody of loneliness and the long crawl.

And then, presto! life is on the move again, the curse is lifted, the obscene shell lies there, the human stands free.

Maybe moral awakening *is* a miracle. Maybe we took it for granted, other times, when the revulsion against war raced through the nation like a tidal wave, sweeping the warmakers off their feet and out of office.

One had almost forgotten, not hope, but the aura that surrounds hope, a nimbus, a light around life, the overflow, the free and lofty gift that made all easy, made light, literally, of loss and sacrifices.

That sense of things comes back once more. It gets born, it is frail as a red infant, must be cherished and warmed, it has but the skin of the newborn to live in the world.

But it is strong, too, and must not be suffocated with inane ordinances, a summons to prudence, underrating the awakened human sense, our only and irreducible resource. Let it go, urge it further, exemplify it, embody it, give it scope and breadth, join it to its proper lineage of heroes and saints and the wise of the earth.

For without that sense, a lightning bolt loosed in us, without that sense electrifying the scattered bones of the wasteland, without it we die more terribly than we have died before. We die the "second death," damnation, extinction.

We have come so nearly to that state as to turn the hardiest soul to water. Which shall we choose? A second death, or a second Coming? We have so nearly chosen wrong, we are so near today, to choosing wrong, the Beast over Christ, death over life, the hideous bomb over the fecund peace—one can only loose an explosive cry—May God be merciful to us!

◁ ○ ▷

We were driving to Point Reyes one day in the brilliant sunshine, a friend and I. We picked up a hitchhiker, a young fellow of twenty or so, blond, well-mannered, quiet of mein. He began, as I understood later, by casing us out. Handed a book over the seat, "a current interest of mine." It was a vivid pictorial account of U.F.O.'s. Then he recognized me, and a light went on in his face: "Aren't you. . . . ?"

He began to talk, urgently; he was going a few miles down the pike, he had so much to tell us. It developed he was about to fly to Brazil, "to the upper Amazon, to join a tribe of nearly extinct pre-Mayan Indians." And why?

According to our passenger, these poor folk had been visited centuries ago by outer space people. "And their message got into the sacred books of the tribe. The books warn of a universal catastrophe around the year 1981. These people are to be the sole survivors."

And by what means would they survive? He was so calm,

possessed, his eyes slightly dilated (but whose aren't these days?). He was telling the least likely, the most outrageous goings on, in an atonal, almost priestly voice. And the sun shone, and we careened on in our van, in and out of the great dewy shadows of the redwood. All as usual, and all apocalyptic. "They were instructed by their outer space brothers to build all dwellings underground. And this they have done."

We came to his destination. But he wanted more time, he said. Could we not listen awhile? So, we stopped the van at a place he designated. I questioned him, he seemed to want to be questioned. What did his family think of such a project? He shrugged. "They let me do what I must do." Like all his statements, this one came out flat; he might have been reporting on the weather or the landscape.

"And will you be in touch with your family from the upper Amazon?"

"There's no way to be in touch with anyone, outside the tribe."

I pushed matters a bit, "And how long will you stay with them?"

"Oh, forever, all my life."

It was that way of the young, to announce stupendous moves, the undertaking of heroic vows, journeys to the edge of the world. And all in a tone that underplays, and thus underscores; high seriousness, noble purpose, the madness that redeems.

I remembered. This was the way, in another time and world, I announced to my family that I was "going away to be a Jesuit." And one day a few months later, when all were apparently acclimated to my going, toward a land fully as exotic as an Amazon (we being country people, people on the land)—it struck me full force, that announcement of mine. Struck me with the physical force of a blow, self-inflicted. I was giving away my life, everything, the future, family. I was going into inaccessible places, into the unknown. Never again would I be among those I loved in the comfortable shabby old house where life was survival run, a free-for-all. My brothers and parents would be visitors from other places, we would breathe different air. And I would be homesick as a driven dog. It tolled in my head; it was forever, there was no turning back.

It comes to me again, as it struck me that day. It was 1939, I was in a darkened movie house, the bell tolled. I sense the darkness, how thick it was! And I wept there for the renunciation that lay ahead, never to be revoked (not revoked, come hell and high water, to this day).

This struck me about our young hitchhiker, a sense, however strange and ill-founded and wrong of head, a sense of vocation. The gyrovague trudging, flying, to the edge of the globe. As I had done.

But with what a difference! For we must not romanticize the matter. We tried, my friend and I, not to dissuade our young passenger from his wild voyage. It would have been useless in any case. But apart from tactic, there was a deeper question. Could he connect with the real world, with us? We spoke of our having been arrested a few days previously at the university, demonstrating against nuclear research. We spoke of our need to assuage the suffering of people, here and now; we felt this was our slim chance for survival.

He listened, his courtesy was impeccable. My friend urged the case. Could he not come to Berkeley before his departure, for a more leisurely converse, a meeting with friends?

No, there could be no question of telling others of his intent. Secrecy was imperative, for the tribe was endangered, and his being received by them was strictly on a confidential basis. We understood. (I understood, for the purpose of persuading. Beyond that, I was at sea.) But could he not come anyway, and look us up? At the very least, he must know that we would do what we could to speed his purpose. And with that he left. We passed him, he waved and smiled, and that was all. Down that road, the young back, the blond poll, pure California, shortly to be airborne, twice born, the angel of the upper air, into the empyrean, young Icarus nearing the sun. . . .

And flew away, away from registration, and draft, the accursed progress of the death culture. Away, away. From the nukes and their makers, the unmakers of youth, the narrowing vise, the claim on the shoulder, Mars at the door.

Off to join the space folk, the only survivors. One of the young, who see themselves only as survivors, or nonsurvivors. Not as artists or poets or healers or singers or defenders of the victims or teachers of little children or magicians in pursuit of the illusive human. Survivors. The underground. The outer-space people. The gnostic quest.

Despair? He had incardinated despair, he had all but exorcised it, he had levitated, grown wings. This world meant nothing to him, let it go its way, its damnation was no business of his, in quest of purity and salvation as he was. Bombs and bucks, what were these to him?

Sitter on pillars. Desert father. Hermit, fleeing the world, its enticements, sirens, appetites. He was chaste as a Galahad, the grail went before him, the pillar of cloud. Farewell, farewell.

God grant him sanity, God grant him something better than California, than the fifty States of Amnesia, than America. God grant him friends who touch and assuage and cherish. God grant him a life a notch above survival. God grant him the sun, and eyes to see it, and a fate better than the curse of underground and outer space; whence we have driven him, insane as we are, and condemning the young to such measures as he laid before us that day. . . .

Let me grant for a moment, for argument's sake, that our young Seigneur has come on a truth stranger than fiction, a truth beyond myth. Grant him his tribe of endangered beauties, his saviors from space, their books, the impending catastrophe. Grant him all that; I want to. And that granted, let me say something about the difference between his journey and my own.

Truthful or not, his is romantic; the most I can grant it is the quality of romantic truth. The truth is the truth of our common lot, for whether in 1981 or after or sooner, we are in for it, and need no sacred books to tell us, but only a simple scan of daily events. Our future is our present, which is to say, catastrophic.

No, it is not in this we differ, he and I. But it is the journey, where it leads, what purpose governs it; these make all the difference. And I propose that even if my friend reaches his buried world at the edge of the world, and burrows in with the others, and survives there, he still is far from the truth he crossed the world to engage. Meantime, my friends and I plug along the Street named Improbable.

Grant, we pray, that we reach the end of that road.

I know that ending, I have seen it in nightmares. There is a barrier, ahead, a dense underbrush, only the shadow of a path, and that named Impassable. Let us go on.

10

We have not been taken seriously on the issue of nonviolence (I restrict my reflections here to my Latin American friends and their North American disciples.) Obviously, the question as it applies south of the States is a very thicket of complexity. And one could hardly expect seriously the exporting wholesale of our anti-war and civil rights experiences.

However, the point is that we continue to offer a serious religious resistance to war making, American style. We have been at this task for some fifteen years or more, always in conjunction with a discipline of prayer and sacrament. And further, we are convinced that the fundamentals of this work are applicable to any culture and time.

Or so we believe.

Others obviously have serious reservations in the matter. Word has even reached us to the effect that our nonviolent resistance is looked on as a kind of government tool, quite acceptable and even useful to evil authority, that our nonviolent ethos plays into guilty hands, puts a religious patina on the gun metal. Whereas if we were only to take up the guns ourselves, the religious guns. . . .

A more glaring misapprehension of our work could scarcely be imagined. Indeed, those Latin theologians who arrive in the States, invariably to teach and lecture in universities and seminaries, remain quite ignorant of the nature of our work. Themselves innocents abroad, they show little enthusiasm for seeking out the communities that exist at some distance from the great "learneries." Who of them has sought us out, the Catholic Worker groups in some thirty cities, the religious resistance communities, Quakers, Evangelicals, Catholics? We never see them, they lecture in liberation theology, and depart, quite ignorant of events and lives beyond the clipped acres of academe.

In such wise, the Latins judge us without meeting us; and the North Americans concentrate on theologies developed outside their (and our) borders, their and our culture, problems, forms of violence. Strange.

◁ ○ ▷

I think nonviolence is the nub of the difficulty; this sticks in the craw.

I think there is little patience in America with a version of the gospel that urges us to prefer giving our life to taking life.

I think the American ethos swamps the gospel and rides it under like a great tide a low dwelling. We put at a distance the question of violence, and therefore the question of nonviolence; neither question quite arrives on our doorstep. It is always guns in principle, guns as legitimate option, talk of guns, dream of guns, tactical guns. The guns are supremely useful tools. They are never discharged here and now (the revolution never quite arrives, here and now). But they fill the time, the void, the attention and imagination. They are, in fact, as are the nuclear weapons, both lethal and abstract; eminently fitted, hand-in-glove, to the culture, which seldom is obliged to look on its victims, and so remains at peace with murder. Let us have the guns, let us persuade ourselves that the gospel allows us to have them. Perhaps, who knows, they will never be discharged. Perhaps.

Such divagations allow the real questions to be indefinitely shelved. Like: what might be the potential for decent social change, if nonviolent action and theory were seriously pursued by Christians? Such action as was pursued, for example, by the Buddhist community of Vietnam during the worst years of the Saigon regimes, such action also as brought the Shah of Iran to his watery knees, and in Afghanistan seem to be stopping the Soviet monster in its tracks?

We know nothing of such matters, we brush them aside impetuously, if not with contempt. Such methods are for other cultures, other faiths (we cannot well add the third member of the triad of clichés, "other times"; since such movements are embarrassingly present in our own times. But let that be.) Meantime, a violent church and its craven leadership is quite prepared to bless and push another military outrage; witness the Catholic bishops' approval of draft registration.

◁ ○ ▷

I call blood the "unforgivable fluid."

Everytime we pour blood, on draft files, on doorways and portals of the Pentagon and its think tanks and laboratories, the media cringe as though they themselves lay under the spray. Including the religious media. They refer to "red liquid" or "red substance" or "purported blood," or "animal blood." I have even read, "red ink."

Now it would seem a fairly simple project to verify our claim that the liquid poured was, indeed, human blood, our blood—there are, I am told, laboratories available for such forensic or journalistic needs.

Something more than a mere slippage of style or facts is occurring here.

It has to do with fear, a taboo, recoiling from a reality too dramatic, too hot to handle.

On the one hand, blood is infinitely cheap in Pentagonal eyes; Americans shed blood all over the world, and make light of it. But when blood is freely given, wasted, a gesture of mad largesse and moral urgency, a counter blood-letting—then it becomes awesome, awful, unbearable. What are these crazies up to, anyway?

No wonder the circumlocutions, the fits and starts and feints and consistently wrong reporting, even more, the consistent news blackout of our actions. For we are not "news"; we are merely good news. And that is another matter entirely. In such times, it means: fractiousness, anarchy, disorder. It evokes nightmares, a nightmare of truth, a haze of blood on the air.

Let us by all means mumble our Bibles and clog the airways and tubes with a welter of religious smog. But enact the Bible? Never.

◁ ○ ▷

A most vexing question, which seems to evade sound solution to this day, is: How much truth do we owe them?

"Them" being the authorities and courts and jails, our adversaries and sentencers and disposers, those who take us in charge in the course of the peaceable struggle, and presumably execute justice on us.

A more profitable way of putting the question might be: How much truth do we owe ourselves, and each other?

Every one of the classical truth tellers I've read or met seems quite scrupulous in raising the question, sweating it out.

It should be said, without serious cavilling, we owe at least a higher standard of conduct than theirs displays. In this regard, we walk or swim, or trim sails, or founder, between a veritable Scylla and Charybdis. On the one hand, a merely tactical view of the truth, or the substitution of a code of good manners for the truth itself. On the other, a flat statement; we owe them nothing, they are the doers of evil, the enemy of humankind. To presume any debt here is to mistake the issue, which is the survival of humankind, our singling out the adversary, our concentrating on methods and means, etc., etc.

In the midst of all this, it should be acknowledged as clearly as possible, we owe a debt of truth, first of all, to one another.

The integrity of our movement, its character as alternative to the lying, feinting, moral squalor which is a staple of public conduct—this is of the essence.

But what of "them?"

The term is useful, it seems to me, only if we are speaking of the adversary as official job holder, wielder of clubs, macho authority, power broker. Certain officials are, by definition, our declared opposite numbers. Their stance, the decisions they arrive at, the odious fallout they loose on all sectors of life today—these tend to set up clear lines, a "we" and a "they." So the questions are clarified, to a degree. But only to a degree. We must not lose our human sense, the truth of alternative character and conduct, by allowing such abstractions unchallenged play.

For our adversaries are also fellow- and sister-humans. Must we not add: We are among the few capable of making the statement in a way that is insistently moral, that will not give up. This is the life and death view, the beyond "the job" view; dare one say, the Christlike view?

In any case, who else is to announce such a view? Who else will vindicate a humanity all but lost sight of, in the furious race of bullish ego and money and power on the rampage that describe corporate and political life today?

Maybe we are a little closer to seeing our question in the round. Acknowledging a debt of truthfulness, not reneging on promises, refusing to act in secret. (Jesus: "I have spoken openly to the world; I have always taught in synagogues and in the temple, where all Jews come together; I have said nothing secretly. Why do you ask me? Ask those who have heard me, what I said to them; they know what I said.") These, it seems to me, are ways of summoning to the bar the humanity of our adversary.

We owe the truth a debt. We owe our humanity to others, even to the inhuman. Perhaps the debt is largest, and least often paid, in that direction.

If not we, who? The question came home to me vividly in a

cell in the Washington, D.C. jail, whence we had been posted after an anti-nuclear demonstration.

We put the question this way: What should be our attitude toward the authority that continually deceives us, conceals its intent, raises the ante on human survival, wastes the earth, jails those who resist?

Philip said simply, "I think we are their only hope."

Indeed. What other access do they have—to life, to the truth of the terror that possesses them? What other hope, than those who risk freedom for the endangered truth?

To go on, hearkened or ignored, effective or despised, to go on as an evident truthful alternative, this is the task.

◁ ○ ▷

I feel as though history were hot on our heels. March 3, 1980, fifty of us were arrested at the Lockheed plant of Santa Cruz. The arrests followed on three days of intensive planning and leafletting of households, stores, and offices of the area; on the last day, we tried to enter the plant to speak with the workers. Heavy police presence, stolid civilian "security" folk, all the paraphernalia of centers where the death egg is guarded, incubated. It was an old story, always new; new in the faces and enthusiasm and insight of those taking part. Come, Holy Spirit.

They threw us, men and women separate, into great concrete caverns, windowless and filthy, an eerie single bulb glowing overhead. There we cooled heels and summoned such good humor as we could for such hours, while they debated our fate.

Then an announcement: We were released, all charges dropped. A sense of letdown momentarily, as though some high purpose had been thwarted in mid act. And then, we gathered our wits and belongings, a more sensible spirit emerged; almost a Buddhist sense. For we had done what could be done. And that was all the Buddha or the Christ would require of us on that day when the Bomb, too, shall stand judged.

We gathered downtown in the noon sunshine, and held our caucus. A good and serious spirit, the healing light overhead. And finally a decision, to let things go for that day, and return in April for another try.

It was a modest and sensible proposal. Down the through-way to Seminary Hill with that peculiar mix of exhaustion and exhilaration that mark such days.

◁ ○ ▷

The scene is a meeting between Gandhi and a young tailor in a small village near Poonah. Gandhi thought of the youth, as he admits, as "one of those impetuous ones who do not think before speaking." The tailor came to talk to Gandhi of the needless humiliation of the poor who traveled the railroads third class (something with which Gandhi was well-acquainted). Gandhi continues the account:

"I had little inclination to talk because of a fever, and tried to finish with a brief reply which took the form of a question: 'Are you prepared to go to jail?'

"He replied with firm deliberation, 'We will certainly go to jail, provided you lead us.'"

Gandhi, like Christ, like Socrates, has a tack of answering a difficulty by posing a question of his own. It is a very old and honored way of getting to the truth. The questioner commences under one expectation; but the answer is a non-answer, it sails in like a curved ball, the surprise is at the tail.

But the surprise is not only in the skill of the guru, it is also in the heart of the youth; for Socrates also has something to learn, as does every "experimenter in truth." He finds, to his delight, that the answer befits the new question; that the moral stature of the youth has stretched to the height of the demand posed. And then the answer whizzes back, curve for curve. He will go to jail, no difficulty, but the guru had best be prepared to come along.

We have here an exchange which I find stunning in its brevity and thoroughness, as though a short story by Chekov or O'Faolain had been further refined, to the scope of a Japanese haiku. No sterile cynicism here, à la Pilate: "What is the truth?" (as though the truth were accessible to his sort of power). But a quest of great purity, valor and persistence on both sides, the older man probing, the younger quick as a whipstock, testing the nimbus about the head of his mentor.

Talk about the suffering of the innocent may be vague (it usually is) or concrete (as in this instance of the young man who sought Gandhi out). In any case, the suffering will go on, a stalemate of injustice, tyranny, and moral lassitude, as long as the talk remains talk. The task of the guru is not merely to sharpen an issue (which seems here possessed of its own keen edge and actuality). It is to shift the *issue* to the area of praxis, where it properly belongs. Let us add immediately—where it belongs on both sides—the older man by no means claiming exemption from the action he recommends to the younger.

Exemptions, they are worth pondering. Buber writes that almost any conscientious person recommends at some time, some action by someone. But it is always someone else—the chief of a state, or the head of a church. "But almost no one says what he himself is prepared to do." Exactly.

"Motilal [the young tailor] captivated me," Gandhi adds. And well he might.

It is the mutuality of conscience that delights, the aged or mature not laying burdens on the shoulders of the young, burdens that properly belong on the shoulders of all. Burdens which, placed on many shoulders, thereby become bearable. "My yoke is sweet, my burden light." It is the Lord who speaks, but the yoke and burden are named, not "yours," but "mine." This is sound instruction, which does not leave the instructor unchanged.

An exalted friendship issues from such episodes, when, across age and experience, a common humanity declares itself, a common task. For many years now, my brother and I have had just such access to young people (freer access, it should be added, than to those our own age). They have found a will on our part to go to jail along with them. We have put demands on them which we never hesitated to heft to our own shoulders. Thus, the friendship became the very opposite of a con game or copout on either side. I am glad for this.

◁ ○ ▷

The Holy Spirit builds the soul in not one, but two, directions. The first is an unassailable sense of rightness at the core of conscience. ("We shall overcome" means, in a tempestuous world, "We shall not be overcome.") This gives consistency and continuity, like good bread and its leaven; same bread, same sweetness and substance all through.

Then outward. The opposite of ego. Which is to say clumsily, serviceability. The bread is good bread, and precisely for that reason, it is meant to be broken, shared abroad. And this is not a matter of grudging diminution. Good bread declares in odor and taste and texture, I am for you. Take and eat.

◁ ○ ▷

Signs of the times.

The world is illiterate in the signs of the times, illiterate even in the signs it fabricates; it does not know a lie for a lie, much less a truth for a truth.

It is literate only in casting up an endless series of clichés and stereotypes; which are not signs at all, but dead ends, a history of deceit and death, a rote babble of dead souls.

Nuclear signs?

They are presented as wonders, portents, inspiring awe, paroxysm of dread, paralysis of will, helplessness. Derangement of conscience, trivializing of life. Style bereft of death.

Add to these, dread of life, wilfulness, violent outreach, communities breaking like dry sticks.

But this is not all. The power of Jesus dispels the chimera.

11

Every prior folly had been reparable. Every prior war could count on survivors, the hideouts, the aged, the children, to carry on. Even though the best had perished. Whether by gun or by resisting the gun. But, willy nilly, no catastrophe ever reached round the globe, threatened to crack it open like a hazel nut in a pincers.

Nobody. No survivors. No children. No flora or fauna.

There was a time before time, by analogy. We were advised once to think of it, to imagine it, as an exercise in prayer, the pure and total self-contained existence of God.

Now let us conjure up a time after time, a day after the last day. A way of imagining the last day; not a sacred Return, but a mad, secular apocalypse. Thus one might place the soul and its despairs in a more salubrious and sober perspective.

For if our future is nothing more than the extrapolation of present methods, politics, war budgets, church conduct—then it must be said quite simply that we have no future at all. Such a future is the extinction of any future; it is a wipeout, annihilation. And it must be noted that such a non-future is being planned, soberly, icily, on a daily basis. It is also being acceded to, in an onslaught of despair, by multitudes of citizens.

In this sense, we are facing something utterly new under the sun. Humans have had to cope before this with inhuman conditions, overlords, and so on. But the human task has never before had to confront the stony unlikelihood of any future at all. We have not been prepared to face a cosmic suicide drift, much less to turn it around. Especially when the anomie issues, not out of discernable malady, loss, physical misery, destitution of goods—but afflicts precisely those who, according to the canons of consumerism and imperial appetite, have "most to live for."

◁ ○ ▷

The doggedness and irascibility of the Pentagon workers. (I include here the whole range of job holders, from the pushers of brooms to the pushers of bombs.) It is like all America is under one canopy of doom.

The anger that flares out at us is easily explained. It is the concentration, in one place, of the ill will and sourness and ungraciousness that mark practically everyone today. The pressing of the lees. (But the first pressing is hardly more palatable.)

Everyone is working for America, but America is not working for anyone. The *double entendre* here is of import; what do you do with your life when your life is irretrievably stuck?

Answer: Your choices are narrow, but there are still choices. You either (1) stop living, thus adding another corpse to the ethical ossuary, or (2) you get unstuck, you walk out on the death scene, responsibly.

Most people, of course, find the second choice as remote as a galaxy, a non-impinging fact, so to speak. And thus, inevitably, they line up for the first choice; military registration, then induction. And thus goes our fate.

◁ ○ ▷

Civil disobedience ought never be a substitute for unsatisfactory lives. Civil disobedience is the natural flowering of satisfactory lives; those who grow concerned grow quite naturally to deeper concern, and so to steps that dramatize their conscience.

On the other hand, crazy jobs drive people crazy; and crazies are not helpful members of resisting political or religious groups.

Along these lines, I find in the seminary that the people most apt for political risk-taking are already in touch with other lives, exerting a certain moral influence. These lend a certain weight, even grandeur, to a politically hot scene. They have already been there, and endured the heat.

Something of this comes through, in contrast, in the yelling that greets us at the Pentagon and elsewhere: "Go get a job, you crazy b-----s!" Once you meet the yell with the fact that you *do* have a job, that you earned the right, and the transport, and the breakfast that brought you there, things tend to simmer down. Whereas, if we were welfare "cases," we'd have to get past that one, too.

If people's lives did not stir up in them a sense of absurdity and panic, anger at others living "off the fat of the land" wouldn't occur. Let alone anger toward those living off the "thin of the land," a more accurate description of the present dole.

The yell is, in fact, a cry for equal misery. We're stuck, why should anyone be unstuck? Especially when the unsticking (this is the heart of the grievance) doesn't include us! More, why should we have to pay for the solvent that unsticks others, but won't unstick us? . . . It all gets enormously complicated, labyrinthine, like the hideous Pentagon itself.

◁ ○ ▷

I don't want to be dogmatic about the above reflection. Touching our experience, civil disobedience is an option for everyone today who can read the bold print of events. Short of such acts, I tend to think there aren't many satisfactory lives left; at least such lives won't long survive. Meantime, the ground shifts and erodes underfoot, this occurring with catastrophic speed to the elderly, the poor, the unemployed. But occurring to the privileged also, whether they are capable of conscientious understanding or not. The earthquake isn't particular, doesn't care whose feet and bones get shaken; it shakes on. And where or when will we step on firm ground again?

Those whom the military and the corrupt politicos are stealing from most flagrantly, that is to say, those at the bottom of the pit, may take satisfaction in a cold comfort. That is to say, they are tasting first what is proposed as a diet for everyone, sooner or later. Fewer amenities, then fewer necessities. And those who still have choices on such things (bus fare and breakfast) ought to be the ones who speak up for those whose cupboards are already bare.

But this is not occurring. Thin times bring on a very frenzy of cupboard-locking by those to whom hoarding makes a perverse sense.

And the hoarding, and the fear that engenders it, lead in one direction only—down and down to the noisome sub-basement, the ultimate bomb shelter, and the shotgun at the door.

12

We were trying for years to create our first world version of those "communites of the base," that were getting such notice (and rightly so) in Latin America.

We were also "doing theology" instead of merely studying it. That is to say, we were reflecting on the gospel in communities, then showing some measure of political follow-through in public. This went on, both during the Vietnam years, and afterward, when war or the threat of war or a war economy or war fever or war preparation and weaponry—any or all of these, but always war, kept blowing a torrid breath at our backs.

This was the pressing and inescapable task for humans, for Christians, in those years of our Lord that were in effect becoming the Years of the Bomb, our true lord and master.

Need one add, the task was not easy? Let me say it anyway, it was all damnably difficult, and required (of others far more than of me) such patience and long sufferance as would make Job rub his eyes in disbelief, or pure joy, or both.

There were, meantime, two difficulties that prevented the liberation theologians and their American enthusiasts from taking us seriously. We were, first of all, nonviolent in principle and tactic, and secondly, we were not particularly interested in a Marxist analysis of current society. These were sins against the Liberation Code. They were not to be tolerated, and we were written off without a hearing.

I must insist that I remained good friends with Guttiérez and Paolo Frière, and worked in tandem with the latter on occasion. It was a cause of astonishment to me that I could call him friend, and yet be at odds with the American students of his thought. Here was something passing strange indeed; they seemed to me dogmatic and rigid, he was supple of mind and good humored.

As to the nonviolence issue, I hesitated mightily whether to allow our differences to be aired in public. I sensed that Frière felt the same reluctance. We both sensed, from far different points of view, that the "debate" we were being urged to enter was a trap. What North American Christians needed above all, was not a public spectacle on matters of differing ideologies— an event that would leave the heart of the problem untouched and lives sailing serenely on in dangerous waters.

What needed confronting was precisely North American violence, the violence of our lives, appetites, instincts, institutions; our carnivorous, even cannibalistic, conduct in the world. Here was the rub; it was rubbing others raw, flaying them alive.

For this reason, as I recall, Frière and I, without prior agreement, but by a kind of instinctive feel for things, stopped the show. We kept insisting in what ways we could devise on the accountability of North Americans—for CIA crimes, nuclear arms, the waste of arms budgets, the torture academy where Latin American police were trained, the voracious multi-corporations. Such considerations were not well received, as may be imagined.

Then there were the Christian-Marxist study groups, in which I had a brief (very brief) experience. It happened in this way; one such pioneer group was planning a weekend on Marxist-Christian theory and praxis; to Detroit, therefore, was I invited.

About what ensued, I will not be overlong, as the event can by now mercifully be relegated to ancient history. Let me only say that the atmosphere of the gathering was rigid and didactic. One would indeed have thought himself marooned in some Moonie bootcamp or Stalag. There were methods and suppositions in the air that I, for one, found repressive and even punishing; we were shunted tonelessly from place to place on the split second, surrounded by acres of newsprint on the walls, upon which every least suggestion of the group must be recorded. I, and others, were finally arranged in something called a "fish bowl," surrounded by 360 degrees of audience. It was bizarre in the extreme, inhibiting to the spirit.

I put up with this for some hours, then took resolve and arose to invite the participants who might wish to partake, in a less totalitarian environment, to another form of give and take. Let us assemble on the lawn, I suggested.

A large number, perhaps one third of those present, walked out. And our rump group, chastened and liberated at last, greeted each other with perceptible relief. We undertook on the spot to create our own agenda, breathing more freely.

On Sunday, another minor earthquake. A Eucharist had been planned, to include in its course the taking of communion and some gesture of friendship offered one another, an embrace or handclasp. But some demurred; they refused either the gesture or the communion, or both. They felt, it was explained, that such a service was peddling cheap reconciliation; to show such gestures was only to connive in hypocrisy.

Now it seemed to me that we had reached a theological crux; indeed, a point of no return. The supposition of the protesters, as far as could be discerned, was that reconciliation awaited a stronger will and effort than we had shown. And since such will and effort were so obviously lacking, and given the fate of our brothers and sisters in many parts of the world—we had no right to "act as though" such reconciliation were a *fait accompli*.

Thus, at a Marxist-Christian workshop, was Christianity downed. Something referred to as a "sociopolitical" conclusion was reached—a conclusion with which I would concur with all my heart, as long as one did not call it theological.

Beginning with myself, American Christians are indeed retrograde before the enormous suffering of the world's innocent ones. We are even perversely "reconciled" to such suffering. Our complicity and cowardice block the true reconciling act of Christ. *Nostra culpa*.

All this said, something more must be said. That something more I take to be the heart of the matter; I mean, without which the matter has no heart. I refer, of course, to the

Christian belief that in Christ we are already reconciled. This is, as we used to say, "of the faith!" This is the noble and serene *opus operatum*, the gracious gift of our Lord, given even to his murderous tribe; given moreover in the very heat and clash of their murders.

The matter should be put thus simply and baldly. Either we are already one body; or we are casualties, amputees, corpses of history, sprawled among all others who die in their blood, stained with the blood of their enemies.

So we must swallow, all our lives long, the irony Christ holds out to us—an irony that is, in fact, our only hope. Or we turn away from it, nauseated at the spectacle of our crimes. In which case, no communion, no gesture of peace; a choice stops the heart in its tracks. . . .

Do we not have here a taint of the ancient pelagianism; the human act that preempts God with assertive human virtue? I would think so. In such a view, the saving gesture of Christ is lost in systems of worldly virtue, is subsumed there, becomes effectively (or ineffectively) inducted into a human system of justice on the march; or of justice stalemated. But in any case, the supposition is that humans make history. And let Christ look to himself, for He stands in second place, an ikon or bidder or exemplar, but hardly the heart of the world, the first horseman of history.

I return to an old formula, and apply it anew. If He has not reconciled us in His blood, without us, and turned to us before ever we turned to Him—then we are still in our sins, and shall be. Without His reconciling blood, I believe we shall never reconcile. Indeed, we will end on an ash heap of the world, ashes unreconciled, scattered to the winds of heaven.

We had best take seriously a truth that has been freely offered, unpalatable as it may be, and unsatisfactory to our Promethean skulls, Marxist or Christian or whatever. That is to say (and I speak for myself and a few friends), we had best choose, in shame and confusion, to stand at the altar, and take the bread in unsteady hands and turn and reconcile with our brothers and sisters. This is perhaps the best we can do (the worst being in no need of description here).

On the principle perhaps that an undeserved bread is better than none at all, and a half-hearted gesture better than a heart of stone.

The principle of the lesser evil? Perhaps, better, the principle of the imperfect good. Or the perfect good, imperfectly apprehended.

And because the alternative to all this is simply being stuck where we are, in a world of torture and mass murder. And this is horrible beyond bearing.

I remember vividly the brothers and sisters who that day refused me, and the bread that was offered. I hope the above words may be taken as reconciling ones, words taking in account their consciences, which burn with rightful indignation at the crimes of Christians. But the crime, I insist, is not all; for if it were all, we are still in our crimes, our hope dead on its feet.

No, let us hope on.

II

Ten Commandments
for the Long Haul

1. Love Your Enemies, Love One Another
(Matthew 5:44; John 15:17)

Beyond doubt the two commands, "Love your enemies" and "Love one another," differ in almost all respects. Issued on different occasions, to different auditors.

The command to make of enemies friends, uttered in the course of a long "sermon," crowded with examples, contingencies, ironies, unexpected turns and twists of mind; stern, and final, too.

On the other hand, a far different command: to make of friends, better friends. And this command marks an hour of great solemnity, it is a legacy to a few friends, a restricted circle of those He stands by, who stand by Him to the end. (By supposition, that is, though the outcome in His case is quite different.)

As to the love of enemies, the command indicates that a

people the world once laid claim to is called to be transformed. The world's claim is cancelled. And the scene (at last the setting conveyed to us) is a mountainside, a multitude, friends and strangers, even enemies, scattered about indiscriminately, a random throw of fate, a crowd. Aware and unaware, attached to one another or deliberately distancing, the occasion of their clotting by no means convivial in the common sense of the term. The magnetic force bringing them together being quite simply the presence of a rabbi who beckons and heals, who speaks His mind with power and vehemence.

"I will call you friends." We are told that those who gathered on His last evening did, in fact, become a closer brotherhood. But not easily or cheaply. They first abandoned Him, betrayed Him, denied moreover, that they knew Him, fled in as many directions as their cowardly hearts appointed.

There was a price on the friendship He had invited them to, a friendship that was not according to this world. The price was His own death; and from it they shrank in utmost fear, variously connived, agreed in silence. We are told that they came together again, eventually, in their own blood. But they were no comfort in His death.

Concerning enemies and ourselves, there is a longer, bloodier history. To this day, which is shot with blood.

Let us say only that, despite all, the enemy remains the enemy; and to him, we are the enemy. And this is the way the world goes, a wheel to which "we" and "they" are bound, inexorable as the turn of the world or the outcome of our lives. Murder is the oldest enterprise in the world, just slightly less ancient than creation. And new, new as the latest nuclear horror.

More: the murder is invariably an act of brother against brother. What different meaning could one reasonably attach to the story of Cain and Abel? The one hated the other; and for no good cause (there can be no good cause) he slew him. He slew his brother according to the simplest and most rational process in the world. Because his brother, although he was brother and therefore bound by sacred and strong ties—his brother insisted on being "another," with his own conduct and stance. This stubbornness, although lovable in the eyes of God, was hateful in the eyes of the brother; that Abel would not be absorbed, not buckle under. And more: that his refusal to do so would win favor in the eyes of God. Favor, that is, because God found Abel godlike. He recognized in Abel a way of being creaturely, filial, that won approval.

By a reversal at once tragic and infinitely typical, the brother was degraded in the eyes of his brother. Abel was now the enemy. The bond was cut, the blood ran. It was the reversal of the command of Christ, that the enemy should become the friend. Now the brother (who in principle and in biology is the friend) has become the enemy.

Thus we have the first scene of warfare; the pasture, garden, tilled field—these have become a battlefield. A scene of murder, the simple and brutal definition of a battlefield. Or of an "open city." Or of indiscriminate bombing. Or of a nuclear first strike, or of any strike at all.

I say to myself in bad hours, "If God has become man, and was born and lived and died on our planet, of course He would issue such commands as 'Love your enemies.'" What is shocking, devastating to me (and I would presume, to Him) is that the words could be continually brushed aside, culled and winnowed and learnedly explained away, ignored, badly served. To the point where the plain intent of the words is taken, in most churches, in the writings of most theologians, as plain heresy, or at best, feckless idealism. Indeed, those who would live by such words, and would live in the church, find themselves shunted to the edge, barely tolerated there, made to bear scorn beyond measure.

This must be a matter of mourning wonderment to Christ Himself. As indeed it is to me and my friends, who find ourselves, as I write these words, not merely subjects of state punishment, which is quite natural and predictable. But something more; all but declared personae non gratae in the church, a loss of a quite different order.

I set this down, summoning what good humor I can, a kind of quizzical patience in my guts. I try to trace the mysterious course of the irony. There can be little doubt that a life in pursuit of the admonition of Christ to make friends of enemies leads in astounding directions, brings forth outcomes of stupendous surprise. For instance, one may never succeed in making a friend of a single enemy, over many years. But one will succeed, in the course of an effort commonly known as peace-making, in creating a spiky and thorny forest of strangers and hostile folk. The effort abroad does not help one's situation at home; quite the opposite.

In fact, the effort abroad is often received as an affront at home. It disturbs good order of things, due course, peace under the common roof. It little matters that this course and order are, often in fact, a mask, a grimace, a slovenly surrender; that they reproduce, *in parvo*, the public chaos, duplicity, surrender. I do not know why this should be so; I only know that it is so. I do not know whether it is so through some law of nature gone sour, or of grace badly served. I am by no means sure that it is even worthwhile, given our predicament, pursuing the matter. Let one go like a chastened schoolboy, back to his lessons, there to learn on page one of the Christian Handbook, how the world, including His dearest friends, dealt with Christ. There, of course, the ground opens up, the bottom drops out of all worldly expectation.

Such things said, one had best draw back. For the whole story is not told by such events, such defeats.

It must be added that the task of making enemies friends is a task that can go forward only among friends. This is a part of the whole task we call life. But it is something infinitely more, it is the reward of the task, its consummation.

The beauty of it all but stops the tongue in the telling. How shall I describe the friendships of these years, their milestones, their land and sea marks, a living scripture, the shouts, signs, smiles of life itself?

If the years are bitter, and twist us about dizzyingly, and test us to the utmost, humiliate us and score points against us (our gaucheries, our malice, our broken promises, points rightly scored)—if all this is true, something else is true: the years are sweet to the tongue, to the entire being. Taste and see. Taste friendship, brotherhood, marriage, every good and human thing ripe on the tree of life. Taste the love of children, how precious, rare it is! Can any taste of this world so fill our hearts?

Thus it seems to me the two commands meet, coincide in a richer meld. In making friends of enemies, we also make better friends of friends.

There are few other rewards worthy of us—or indeed offered us. And the reward is ample to overflowing. Let us give thanks for it.

2. Do This in Remembrance of Me

(1 Corinthians 11:24, 25)

Three evangelists record the Lord's instituting the sacrament by which we remember him, but only St. Paul preserves for us the reason. The words have in them a density, an underscoring hardly found in other commands of the Lord.

Can it be that He dreaded above all to be forgotten, His deeds wiped out, the sentence of death so soon to be passed on Him, indeed closing the dossier, the "case of Jesus Christ"?

Such an agonized thought may have occurred, a thought that would pass through the mind of someone in His plight, a cloud across the sun. How terrible to be forgotten! How terrible to sense, before death, at the gates of death, that one's work, one's way in the world, words, images, admonitions, the coloration and style and glance which appear to one as unique, one's own, (one's gift as well)—that these were shortly to be thrust down some hole, crevasse, grave. How terrible to be forgotten! A death before death. As though indeed one's life had become an impediment, an embarrassment, an interruption in the feckless liaison of cowardice and indulgence we call life. That look in the eye of the beholder that says more deafeningly than words—good riddance.

How terrible, on the other hand (it is really the same hand)—to forget. To forget Christ, how terrible for us. I think this too was in the pain and urgency of His cry, "remember me!"

How can we forget Him, and still remember ourselves, remember each other, remember our true place in the scheme of things, the web of life? The thought is ridiculous; more, it is a simple violation of true order. And once occurring (and since it occurs every day) this amnesia which has about it the damp chill of the grave, strikes us dead to the resurrecting virtue of Christ, the strength that issues from Him in healing and constancy of heart.

We are a nation without memory. This is the demonic triumph of technique and the media and the consumer clutch whose prey is the meat of the heart. These assaulting forces set us spinning dizzily above the void. Until the speed of mad days is overcome by the gravity of death, and the spin becomes a tailspin.

The case that occurs to me is a "true" recollection of the war crimes committed by our government in Vietnam in the '60s and early '70s. Such remembrance would include, if genuine, a determination to repent of such infamies by acts of reconciliation and restoration. No such will exists, as we well know.

Deprived of it, we cannot conceive of ourselves, imagine ourselves as moral individuals, as individuals capable of the basest and bloodiest conduct, as well as of the most exalted and heroic. We lack responsibility, we lack dignity. Or, more simply, we lack a sense of ourselves corresponding to a vision opened by Bible or anthropology or enduring literature or the example of heroes of our race.

The result is a series of lurching frenetic spasms in conduct, each more despairing than the last, more irresponsible and violent. From havoc to greater havoc, from war to war. While true understanding would indicate that history offers us lessons, we are teachable. So we could affirm in all truth that we have learned from past folly, are determined to set sail no more in a ship of fools. Whatever the enticement.

Remembering. In my lifetime, in my country, three wasting,

terrible voyages on the SS Folly: World War II, Korea, Vietnam. I write "three wars," but it could be argued persuasively, and has been argued, that there were not three, but one great pounding continuous war, a tide forever rolling, inundating, sweeping all before—claiming, consuming. A mega war, a tidal wave, its energies generated somewhere, at some hidden time, in subterranean darkness of the soul of our race, a nightmare never exorcised, a war waged against reality itself—a war that in reality never ends.

Of only one war was I capable of true remembrance. Of the others, for reasons too far afield to enter here, my remembrance was blocked, inhibited. When a group of us Catholics set out to remember the Vietnam war, to remember it biblically, not as a mortician's effort, not burying the corpses even as we blessed the bombs—but urging in the very fury and travail of the war, that American conduct in Vietnam be weighed, be judged, be resisted—when we did this, it became clear in the blink of an eye that we stood alone.

Because the pressure laid on us to forget, to desist, to lend our silence to the fire storm, this pressure was at least equal to our determination to remember.

Indeed, a pressure so strong, so perfectly consistent, exerted equally by church and state! If we call remembrance a divine activity, the pressures generated by the twin powers, nicely, subtly blended, tending toward civic-churchly amnesia—these can only be called demonic. They are also, for that reason, all but invincible.

To remember past evil is to renounce it. To remember past goodness is to embody it anew.

When one thinks of such things, it becomes clear that our Lord is offering, in His gentle command, a better way, of living, of dying. So His words are nicely poised at the pivot of death-life, where His own example offers direction, heroism, an exalted and lucid sense of Himself. "Offers" is a key word. If He can urge us to remember Him, it is because He has first remembered us. The bread is broken "for us"; the cup poured out "for you and for all." In the highest moment of self-understanding, the largest embrace is offered, an all-inclusion.

Normally (which is to say, from His point of view, abnormally), we stagger about, vacillating between these two (remember, be remembered) missing them both. Self-understanding becomes a caricature, broadly and even cynically drawn by shrinks and gurus, those who glorify something referred to as "consciousness" a mocking parody of altruism, public understanding, moral accountability. Or by those who glorify the American family, a go-getting, self-consuming indentured slave of war and capitalism. Meanwhile, we are dismembered, we drift about in amnesia. There is little self-knowledge, the culture has seized on the clues and destroyed them.

What of true remembrance of others? Competition and cupidity can make of the other a threat, an enemy. Indeed, can one truly remember the one he does not love, the one who, as the cultural charade plays on, becomes the declared enemy, standing in the way of consuming cannibalism? And who therefore must be removed, by "whatever means"?

The Christ who remembers. We are not told directly how determinant His memories of childhood were. We know He had strong family ties, which He was at pains both to keep, and to keep in a rightful place. His loving memories of nature appear again and again in parable form, they are drawn into His moral vision, the very light and hue of conscience.

He remembered the future, His own, first of all. It is truly wonderful as we open the Gospels, to look back on such a life as His; and to note how determinedly and calmly He looks forward. The breaking of bread, the passing of the cup; always in view of, taking in account, looking toward—his death. Indeed, in Him we need pay no facile attention to *"divine powers";* His human powers were of such peak and edge that he knew beforehand the necessary outcome of a life such as His own. He smelled death on the polluted moral air of His time, His own death.

Knowing what was in man, He knew the outcome. The

breaking of bread, the breaking of bones, the pouring of the cup, the outpouring of blood. Such symbols sped like arrows to the heart of reality. Thus, He imagined the future, the outcome, not merely a mad conclusion of a present gone awry (though the present, from the conduct of the powerful, their virulent hatred of Him was certainly awry, as is abundantly clear from the start). The outcome was reasoned toward, anticipated, sensed in His prophetic bones, and even though with trepidation and deep fear—was chosen. He chose the path, therefore the destination; or in the Gandhian sense; the means, therefore the end.

It was not simply that the outcome lay in other hands than His own. It did, and it did not. Insofar as discomfiture, self-interest, seizure of polity, were impervious to His words, bristled at His probing, and finally connived at His removal—to this extent, His fate was in others' hands.

But this is hardly saying everything—or indeed much new. To stop here is to grant all power in heaven or on earth to the executioner—to the barrel of a gun and the fury and fear of the gunman.

There is something far deeper to be probed in the case of Jesus, as in those heroes of our lifetime who have died violently in defense of life. I can only call theirs (and clumsily), a vanquishing freedom. It is a kind of dazzling moral consistency; it is verified at every turn and twist of life, goes its own way, speaks up and pays up, unmasks the seductive lie, keeps good humored under provocation; in fact, lives out broadly and concretely the formula of love in 1 Corinthians 13. But it is almost redundant to dwell on such things, we know the signs.

Finally, the great ones give their lives, tragically, in a blood-ridden moment, they turn aside the malice of the murderer, make of death the sweet and strong and prevailing thing we call martyrdom.

To remember the future, we say, is to imagine it. Not a sordid or unavailing past, hauled forward, cosmeticized, dressed up, a ruffian playing hero. This is the future of the world, as the world is stuck in mire. But God knows no such past, no ineluctable series of events that hold the future in its fist.

The true future? Words fail at the thought of the depth, height, breadth of the promise. Something newly created, a coming. Something, we are told, strictly beyond imagining. "What we shall be, we do not know." A new face, better, a new soul. Something where nothing was; a dazzling, unheard of, unseen, unimaginable reality, existing where before was— nothing. A new someone with respect to whom, in comparison to whom, we are now—nothing (precious as we are, and summoned, and even at present, in our travail and sin, of a surpassing dignity). Out of no one, a new someone; out of the distraught and broken, the beloved community.

I think of the tears and failures attendant on holding a few friends, on discerning the signs, on summoning common symbols, reading scripture, praying together, refusing to bicker and harbor resentment—and more, developing a public conscience in face of the mad nuclear march. How difficult, how seemingly impossible!

And I reflect on Bonhoeffer's insistence that community is primarily a gift of the Spirit, made of no human hands. Let me remember this, as I reach the end of resource, the end of a lifeline, and must pray: Come Holy Spirit!

This I think in desolate hours, is indeed worth pondering. In proportion as the future is imagined only in cultural terms, in the only terms a foreclosed culture has at its disposal, terms which past conduct or a politics of fear or self-serving economics or the voracious military may determine—in just such proportion have we missed the point of the command of Christ—to "remember."

To remember the future, in accord with the command of Christ, is to yield to an act of God. It is, in the old phrase, to "prepare the way of the Lord." To be nonimpeding. To hold no brief, make no investment, in a future concocted by this world. Since that so-called future, insofar as the world even grants itself a future, is simply an expanding dark-throated cornucopia of horrors, seriously planned and deployed; ever worse weapons, an ever more badly misused earth. Rampageous death.

Sometimes we can only stand and wait on Him. It is not merely a sense of drowning or suffocation, the sense that our best efforts are unavailing (though it is also that sense). We cry out at times: who can make peace in such a world? We cry out: if only peacemakers were to rise in legions, if only the best part of us, our best instincts, our most denied love, were to arise, legions of peace in place of soldiers sprung from dragon's teeth!

But these are mere dreams, events beyond our powers: they smack of a peace game aping a war game.

The truth of our plight is something other; short of an act of God, we are where we have been, stuck there. Few in our midst, whether of the fervent hell-bent or the fervent opposition, can offer a vision that entails. We have forgotten—it is embarrassing, discomfiting in the extreme to remember—what a true vision entails. The kingdom of God, the kingdom of peace, is the kingdom of the crucified.

Toward that realm, few run. Indeed, even grudgingly, even with half a heart, few walk.

> Prisoners, pray for us.
> Resisters, pray for us.
> Martyrs, pray for us.

3. Sell What You Possess

(Matthew 19:21 NEB)

The Lord who is Lord of the Sabbath is also Lord of the earth. These are truths which lead us farther than we are commonly willing to go. Who indeed today sets the rules, methods, limits within which conscience might be thought conscientious? Ourselves? We who would make of the earth a huge warehouse and wholesaler for consumer appetite, in charge of which we are appointed to dole out the good of the earth to the "deserving"?

Pharisaism. The capitalist ground rules. Indeed. But

religion? And the Lord of the Deep Breath, the Lord of the Cornucopia, has He other designs, on the earth, on us?

Every argument with God implies, of course, contrary visions. In our scene, the argument runs deep and fast. The young ruler and the Lord of all, they walk quite different worlds, test them, see life differently, exercise dominion or servanthood, show forth that concupiscence of power or that relinquishment of power which are the very bones in motion of the unexamined human or the rigorous divine.

The contentious parties circle one another warily. The rich youth, in strict imitation of his elders, wants one foot in this world and one in the kingdom of God. It is a very old balancing act or high wire act or clown act (except that it is always dead serious). More, the act invariably fails, ends in a tumble, in wounds, in mortification or cynicism—in death.

Still the young man of our story is not dead yet, by a long shot. Nor is he mortified or cynical. Assuredly he is naïve, and clings like a lichen to his pride of place.

But unlike his elders, his heart is not hardened, he is a seeker. And therein lies his salvation, or such nearness to it as he attains.

How indeed describe that hair's breadth of moral difference that comes down on the wrong pan of the scales? that separates this youth from a gospel destiny, from John and Peter and Paul and the others? that sends him away with averted face to his old life, "saddened" with all he had seen, had yearned toward—but could not embrace.

The Lord longs to bathe this youth in the light of His own vision. Not only the vision of God, but a mundane vision, a modest vision, a vision of right order and use and step-by-step knowledge. This, strangely enough, is godlike activity. (And we, too, shrink from it, dread its modesty, its demand that we "take up the cross daily, and follow. . . .")

I know a priest who hitchhikes the roads of California, works in the fields, takes his shelter with the poor in public dorms, eats where he may, leaves the security of religious institutions far behind. "Go, sell what you possess." "Foxes have holes, and birds of the air have nests, but the Son of man has nowhere to lay his head."

It is for neglect of such example and admonition, for weaseling out, for waving them aside with svelte theological shrug, for leaving them to others, for sowing misery in the world where a better will would struggle for equable order, for wallowing at the trough while Lazarus starves at the gates—for these sins and more, our world tumbles about our ears. Crimes against right order, crimes against ecology; too much issues in too little, too much creates not enough.

For all that, let it not be imagined that our story commends an esoteric "religious" strategy for eccentrics. We are simply instructed here in a use-non-use rhythm that, in the long haul of history, has proven sound; at once a rule of salvation, of sound economics, and sane ecology. That all may have enough, some must surrender exorbitant claims. Rulers, especially young rulers, must step down; not because old rulers seldom or never do, but because the rulers of this world, any and all of them, invariably stand on the backs of the poor.

All this, to get heard, must be said by someone to someone, up close. For wealth is essentially, perniciously abstract. There can be no piercing this befogging, rotten veil-of-gold, until one has attended to a voice; a voice not only of renunciation, or even primarily so, but a voice of love. Come, follow me. Then the curtain may be rent.

Still, we must not underestimate the hold possessions exert on the heart. Wealth may be abstract, but it has a clutch of steel. How firm it held in this instance! His possessions ruled the young ruler, he turned away sad. . . .

When I entered the Jesuit order, they read this story to us, at the start of our novitiate days: and by no means *sotto voce*. We were told to ponder the words, and especially to ponder the outcome, as it touched on the young ruler. The implication was as clear as it was comforting; each of us had taken a step this other could not take. And for that, our reward would be great in heaven.

We believed it, with all our fervent, untried hearts. There was a sweetness, a moving innocence about that belief. On the one hand, many of us were better housed and fed by the Jesuits than we had been in our families. The fleshpots were never empty, at times they contained an entrée of startlingly gourmet quality. Yet, as in the way of the young in Eden or in Egypt, we dreamed of heroic deeds, or public disgrace even, of witnessing in the old classical way of the martyrs. The dreams were far more pyrotechnic, heady, than the real thing. Dreams of Xavier, of Inigo in jail, of Campion under the ax—these were ways of imagining our future, they were the foundation stones, airy, celestial, cloudy, of a new creation which was even then, as we believed, our emblematic selves, our city, our destiny.

Alas, alas for the dream, and the dreamers as well. We, those former striplings and athletes of the spirit, are cloddish and middle-aged and of piddling virtue. Moderation is all. We are moderate as a Victorian dole, in faith, hope and charity; we will die in our beds, in the course of nature, we will die of our lives.

How different a thing to act, rather than merely to dream! And let one dare act, how unacceptable is the act to the company of dreamers! How bitter are loneliness, rejection, ill repute, sidelong looks, years beyond the pale of church and state. Like the little scroll the evangelist was bidden to swallow; honey in the mouth, gall in the guts. . . .

The young ruler was not invited by the Lord to embrace a better, higher, more sensible code of conduct. He was not bidden to leave Jewish law behind in order to embrace Greek wisdom. Nothing of the kind. He was invited to embrace the law of the cross; a law, need one add, that already governs the conduct and ethos of the one commending.

The youth is, in fact, in the presence of another sort of "ruler" than himself. The contrast was to have been spelled out later had things gone well; only a hint is offered here, the invitation to renounce all, to "come and follow." The ethic to be revealed? It is indeed ecological, and logical, as well. But all this is for another stage of the journey.

The episode of Jesus and the youth has at times been codified in accord with good sense or expediency or some dreadful cliché like "alternate lifestyle." As though the noble summons to discipleship were a matter of Ben Franklin's worldly shrewdness, a matter of jettisoning a certain portion of the junk and debris of America, or flexing one's muscles for some hypothetical long march.

All this, to put things mildly, is to miss the point. For something far different is in question here; an assault on the dark, unregenerate side of the human heart, by the one who reads all hearts. The heart that would grab its swag and run. That, left to its own instinct, would be, not its brother's keeper, but his murderer. That, at all cost, would play master, create victims, become executioner, tyrant, exploiter—in a word, "Lord."

"The kings of the Gentiles exercise lordship over them. . . . But not so with you; rather let the greatest among you become as the youngest, and the leader as one who serves" (Luke 22:25-26).

In the peace communities of the '60s, '70s, '80s, we have striven to give another outcome to the story of the young ruler. Perhaps even to add ourselves to that small band who "follow." In any case, we pray to "serve," not to "lord it over." Need one add that such a hope cuts across all lives, crosses boundaries, exclusions, heals what is divided, lances open what is falsely healed over? For the glance of Christ rests on us, on the cowardly and alert, the humbugged and lucid of mind, on those who play with skill the game of this world and are therein called its "rulers"—upon those also who seek a serviceable way. And resting on us, the glance heals, discomfits, reproves, blesses, and beckons. No one of us but has felt the power and threat of that glance; have seen some turn away in sadness from that assault on assumptions and ego, seen others transformed into healers and seers and lovers.

A chancy moment, a crisis.

That glance of Christ rests on ourselves. "Jesus looked on the young man, and loved him." That love is no entrance ticket to a rose garden, to an Eden out of sight and mind. It is a call, as Ignatius Loyola put it: "to labor with Him, to suffer with Him, to die with Him." It draws one into a whirlwind of passion and mordant mythology, unleashes great winds of sin and violence, renders one's frame incandescent with a hellish destructive light.

And then, something else. In one's deep existence, no dead ikon of Christ, but a figure bathed in sanguinary sweat, the sweat of a blighted and dying humanity. "Come, follow me."

I sense another presence in that terrible arena. It is the fallen angel of the Bomb. It is the demon named Death, the killer of goodness and health and humanity. Before the disarmed Christ, the enemy comes armed to the teeth; a guided missile, an MX, a neutron bomb, a laser. His claims are loud as the cacophany of hell, he owns the earth, he works wonders, he deceives and enslaves even the faithful. He lays his bloody hand possessively on Christ.

Where does he come from? Lately, from the temples and synagogues and churches; he has invaded sanctuaries, interpreted scriptures, conducted meditation sessions, preached eloquently of patriotism and Western values and the blessings due good citizenship. He has quoted Romans 13, Matthew on Caesar's due, Luke on the temptation of Christ; all, need it be added, from a radically different point of view than that of stricken Christ.

He is so persuasive! So awesome, yet so avuncular, so nicely attuned to the voice that assures us that a little murder is a negligible thing, that a lesser evil is no evil at all, that national security is hardly a cause of shame, that freedom of religion is worth fighting for . . . And are not Christians, after all, people of practicality and good sense, who do not follow half-cocked after any piper, any tune?

The brilliant speech is ended. It is intoned by a personage of moment, a ruler of this world, one whose claims are beefed up with a very demon's arsenal, whose will may at times have been challenged, but never thwarted. Thwarted? His eyes glow, the machinery revs up, the plan is on schedule.

He turns a mocking sardonic glance on his opposite Number. "Now, let's hear a proffer."

A silence long as the centuries' trail of blood of martyrs. A silence long as the eonic patience of God. A silence charged with the stifled cries of the innocent under the altar.

When the Lord speaks, it is for the first time, and the last. A word that creates so that all may in turn create, may speak on their own. A voice of thunder and sweetness, a word that heals. "Go and rid yourself," He says. "Then come and follow."

Such images help us imagine our lives. Images of meekness, of discipleship, of renunciation. Indeed, the images were of such import, so dense, so relevatory of the heart of reality, that neither in the furious '60s, the somnolent '70s, nor the '80s as they opened; never could we doubt that our Christianity would stand or perish, in virtue of these images—images of conflict and calling. We could indeed ignore them or turn from them in dread, settle into professional showcases or religious stereotypes. But finally, we could not. We were stripped naked with the naked One, the sweat of assaulted humanity was on our brow. The future, whatever future humans could claim, was placed in our hands. This is my confession.

The images formed and coalesced, and claimed us. We were one with the sorrowful and stricken One, the suffering Servant, an image ancient and honorable, the human sense of humans. It would not go away. At dawn we called it a nightmare, at least in the beginning; we half hoped to shake it off with a witless routine of day, the soporifics of academe, paper shuffling, credentials, repute, all those silly doodlings of reality which impose like a horny skin on exposed flesh, the superego on the infantile soul. America offered so many ways of not hearing, not seeing, not tasting, not walking, not paying! America was a rogue's school of evasive tacks and twists and ploys; so numerous, so persuasive, so cunning, so amply tried, and tested, so cheaply come by, so religious in over- and undertone!

The sorrowful One would not go away.

We tried the palliatives, applied the charms. That was our history. But He would not go away.

And at length, He conquered. The grand inquisitor, the accuser, fell away to rot. Our adversary fell to pieces like a charred doll under the glance of Christ, a death blow to the archangel of death.

This is the way it was, on the day we were snatched from the circle of death, and got reborn at the midwife hands of Christ. I dare speak so, for my friends, for myself, who were summoned: and for others in our lifetime, who passed with us from America and American Christianity (one and the same, all said)—into discipleship. We escaped the net of the fowler, the culture that ensnares and entangles the heart, that would induct us into doom.

I pray my language is not found intemperate or self-serving. These are mere notes describing an unfinished way. There is more to be endured. We have taken none but the first tentative steps of a child. The rest is in the hands that belong to the eyes that met our eyes; to the voice whose timbre and turn of phrase we know, having heard it once for all.

4. Do Not Be Afraid

(Mark 5:36; 6:50 NEB)

In my experience the question of fear is of first import today: fear and the exorcising of fear. One swallows dry in reflecting on it, cringing under it—the shadow, the undersoul. The Bomb?

Strange, we dread exactly those realities, events, crises that the Bible not only asks us to face, but about which the Bible commands something unequivocal: fear not. Economic insecurity, illness, accident, conflict, war, exile, death: fear not!

Today, all at odds with the biblical command, it seems as though life itself were mounting a great conspiracy of fear. As though, like a knot of animals, beleaguered, threatened with extinction, only those who fear mightily and react violently will survive.

(In recent times, this admission has been known as the Ethic of the Shotgun at the Shelter Door. Unless memory misserves, it was first promulgated by a member of my order, designated as we are by the name of Jesus. And to this hour, it has been quite impossible to announce the approval of the "ethic" by the aforementioned Jesus.)

In any case, in giving up our fears, we evidently are being asked, human pawns in a nuke-ridden age, to give up a part of what we assumed to be our humanity itself. To be human, we are told, is to be afraid. Fear guarantees our survival. But for our fears, of Russians, of Chinese, of Vietnamese, of autos, of storms, of guns, of muggers and looters (the list is very nearly endless, a very litany of Armageddon)—but for fear of these, we would long since have fallen prey to one or another enemy, adversary.

What a downfall this is, what unmitigated catastrophe, to those who cherish and guard above all else the cornucopia of that world we love to name First World!

And what lives we lead in consequence, and what deaths we endure, the deaths being both plural in number, and prior to the main event. And, meantime, how stunted in our resolve, how finicky in self-giving! And how clearly it appears, that our plague of fear arises, not in response to real enemies in obscure places, but to our own disordered and sickly version of the world; from our own souls, captivated, at bay.

The exorcising of fear might be named the great prelude to human activity in the world. A kind of genesis story in reverse, making our way through the thicket inhabited by Cain and his crew, forward (not backward) to an innocence that is won (not inherited), the bitter and costly fruit of experience, especially that of forgiveness.

I have a fear, if I may at this point turn confessional. I fear that the above words, or words to follow, might be taken as merely another effort to psychologize (which is to say, to bend out of shape, to trivialize, to subject to merely human competence) questions which I take to be questions of faith. Such a way of proceeding, I believe, when applied to the deepest fears of the soul, would accomplish little, would end only by immunizing the soul against reality itself. That reality being, in the most rigorous sense, fearful, a fear to be lived with, a consequence of faith.

"How fearful a thing to fall into the hands of the living God." The psalmist is hardly reassuring. His words by no means tell us what we wish to hear; that the world, the nukes, the urban crawl, the stuck subway, the stuck economy, the public lies, the private betrayals—all the welter and woe of life today—that we are not to fear falling or being pushed into these or like voids, pits, tragedies, despairs. Jesus and the prophets take all these and more, into account, and add the capstone, a crushing weight indeed; that the God who creates and saves and lives on in the world, is neither gull nor fool nor eternal victim. He is void and unattainable height and racking breadth and tragedy, all these. And to fall into such hands is, in very prospect, a fear beyond fear.

A dulling of truth occurs and a cosseting of experience when, in such unattainable matters, we stick to merely human competence, when the professionals, so to speak, spreadeagle the human spirit on a dissecting table. On the other hand, there is a broadening of the range of life, including and admitting suffering, enlarged possibility and breakthrough, in the biblical vision.

Something shocking is at work in the culture. The tactic there, including the tactic of culture-mongering religion, being simply to pilfer the language of faith, to display with mockery in the national morgue what belongs to the secret womb. Thus, we have pseudo-religious covenants signed in the White House by mimes and clowns, feverishly trading costumes and masks, the bishops in khaki and the generals in drag. And all prattling witlessly of the "national need," to install and hypostatize fear in a permanent cold war, to bastardize religion, to worship the military gods. It is all a kind of theatre of cruelty, theatre of the absurd, conceived in the third circle of Solzhenitsyn, staged by Ionesco.

There are perhaps other ways of coping today, other visions and versions of reality.

It is instructive to note that the same God who declares Himself fearful, also counsels us not to fear. Indeed.

To fear and not to fear. Perhaps those whose conquest of fear has overcome demons and misfortune and death itself, are ready for the fearful encounter with God. For the same God who reveals Himself as fearful also assures us that He loves us. More, that between loving and fearing, there is no ineluctable dilemma, but a mutuality whose center is indeed warm, a nest, a haven, a roof and walls, a corner of peace. But whose edges are indeed edgy, and do wound.

Such reflections are, of course, quite general. I take them at face value, or try to. But we are also to note where they land, and where take root. Have we, at a point of crisis or loss, tasted that casting out of fear that, we are assured, is both the labor of love, and its reward?

There is a kind of interesting ignorance, both dense and healing, that overtakes one on occasion. It is as though, in an access of light, sudden and intense and concentrated, a light like a whip lash, enough light, so to speak, to allow a single step to be taken—in such a light the faces of assailants, enemies, adversaries, out there somewhere in the dark, these are extinguished, fall back. Something has happened. A light has gone on in the soul. And in that light, the surrounding darkness has become absolute, stygian.

What is this? we ask ourselves, bewildered. I see where I could not see, I walk where a moment ago I stood petrified. And my fears and dreads, that great inhibiting demonic pack—it is still there somewhere in the darkness. But it has fallen back, it fears the fire.

And I can walk. And I walk.

And this is grace.

At other times, it seems as though the counsel "not to fear" makes as little sense as a counsel to the ocean tides to roll back, or a command to the earth to stop in its spatial tracks. Not fear? but that is to stop nature in its appointed round, it is to grow scales and armor, it is to cease touching the world. It is to stop dead, a corpse, an unborn being.

In any case, who can command the emotions of another? . . .

Every time I face arrest, my heart turns over. The fear is so strong at times as to be a matter of physical illness, nausea. I dread the arrest, the shame, the puerile round of handcuffing and fingerprinting and lockup, the immensely boring and absurd ritual of the court. I fear the moment of sentencing, I fear jail. My cowardly heart longs in every fiber to have done with this charade, a game in which no one wins, nothing changes, a chess game played out in a nightmare, no outcome.

You walk with your fear as you would walk with an illness, determined that it will not down you. You cannot deny you are ill, but you will not allow illness to speak for you, or halt you, or trip you to the ground. This I think is a clue; to disallow fear the last word, the word that wins. And on the other hand, to refuse to play superman, as though some improbable exorcism had cast out fear once and for all, and one were walking through fire and smelling roses.

It is good to recall, and chastening to our pride, that before His death, Christ felt the chill of fear, numbing His spirit, invading His bones.

Yet He went forward to death, and conquered. He walked the way of the cross, with His fear, an impediment heavy as the wooden horror itself. And fell under it. And stood again, to the end.

5. When You Are Haled into Court, Prepare No Defense

(Luke 21:12-14)

Despite the admonition, we always prepare, and deliver where allowed, statements to the court: though it must be added that we do so without great enthusiasm, and with care that legal punctilio be subject to our conscience.

Still, what of the admonition?

It must be noted, first of all, that Jesus defended himself.

> The high priest questioned Jesus about his disciples and about his teaching. Jesus answered: I have always spoken openly to the world; I have always taught in synagogues and in the temple, where all the Jews come together; and I spoke nothing in secret. Why do you question me? Question those who have heard what I have spoken to them; they know what I said.

The point of the command seems to be, not so much a prohibition against stating one's case, as an urging to keep one's intent clear. In defending oneself, one's aim is not self-justification, but service of the truth.

A forum in which to state one's case: this is our only point in going into court at all. It also is a clue to our skepticism about the paraphernalia of the legal labyrinth.

In any acceptable sense, I have long concluded that we have no defense to offer. American courts were not set up to offer conscience, enlightened or otherwise, a forum for actions that could only be considered, in legal skulls, subversive of good order. The courts were set up to dispose of criminality, understood as contravention of law. Period.

In such circumstances, one did what one could. The court scene, variously understood by various defendants like us, offered a chance (now and then) to say one's say in public, according to the lights of each. Moreover, one could also, now and then, request a jury trial. That meant that eight, ten, or twelve peers sat through a process that might bring light to one side and relief to another. The relief, be it added, was invariably understood by us, not as our getting off the hook, but as a possibility of bringing a measure of moral understanding to a heavy darkness. The jury, so to speak, might see the light and vindicate the defendants. Or if they did not (they almost never did), perhaps one or another among them might register a change of heart. There was always hope.

So you didn't give up. Or in a sense you did give up; and that proved to be your strength. You gave up on a system that weighed your conscience in its crude scales, never allowed the bandage to be ripped from its eyes. You came to the end of illusion.

And yet you didn't give up on the decency of people. And this resolve included, in an embrace too large-hearted to be entirely rational, even those paid or appointed to "dispose of criminality," including your own. You didn't give up on them, not because of some florid or romantic theory about human goodness (theories that were rather constantly punctured by experience, as they shipped your conscience off to be Americanized).

No, you refused to give up on judges and prosecutors because, after all was said, after all the palaver and debate and objections and briefs and codicils and (above all), ego—because it was clear you were forbidden to do otherwise.

I am writing this with all seriousness, for in this we touch on the heart of several matters. For us, questions of evil and goodness were never to be left in the hands of psychologists or historians or penologists or any others who poke about in deep waters. We were not taking our lead (here's that irrational embrace once more) in our attitude toward those hired to condemn and sentence us, from "problem areas" of the human psyche; and this no matter what light may presumably be shed on those depths and shallows by various skills and competencies. We were not dealing with a problematic at all. We did not think the problem defined the human.

Quite the opposite. And here we parted company with that world which on other grounds we wished to make friends with. We believed that the question of the human was a mystery. That any light shed on that mystery was a gift of God, a revelation. And more, revelation was not merely light turned on dark recesses. More, much more. It encompassed and demanded an act of gratuitous love.

Something else follows, closer to our topic. For such as us, people who see themselves as witnesses on behalf of life rather than spectators at a bloody circus—for such there could be no "defense," as commonly or juridically understood. In the nature of things, there could not be. Our ethic, our vision, our tradition, are essentially at odds with the ethic, vision, political presumptions of the war-making state. We simply stand on other ground. Which is not to elaborate here a claim that ours is firmer ground (we believe it is) or higher ground (ditto).

Simply, for the purpose of these reflections, we walk to a different drumbeat. Its beat is complex. It commands fancy footwork; not merely a different rhythm of life, vision, moral skill, brought to bear on a civilly disobedient act. It demands that, practically, meticulously, civil disobedience be shown to connect with a grander rhythm of conscientious history—a history of sensitivity to the lives, limbs, and spiritual liberty of others. And in consequence, in court, on the stand, in prison, that same history presses on us, a moral follow-through, compounded of strength, plain speech, decent and sensible and (to those of good will) winning conduct.

So, as is known here and there, we joined the criminal class with unseemly enthusiasm, even joy of spirit; and were haled with deliberate speed to a system of justice, impressive in details of staging, props, rhetoric; more than persuasive, positively lowering to the spirit. A court of justice which, due to the abnormal times, the warlike times, the inductive, assertive, voracious times, is to any sane view, a court of injustice. At least in our case (and arguably, in all cases). A court of necessary injustice. Not a merely mitigated injustice, a temporary or occasional one, a slip of the gavel, a slip of the tongue. I speak of nothing so capricious as the buckshot approach to crime and punishment that governs a typical day in a typical court, dealing and wheeling about typical crime.

By no means in our case. But a metaphysically necessary injustice. An injustice at war with justice. At war with its own soul, thrashing about in a net of expediency, racism, political bribery. An injustice which breaks out in the open, though rarely, in a cry, a blank look of pain and loss, as though the practitioners saw their own soul laid on a butcher block, divided heart from head, limb from limb.

Always and inevitably, a court of injustice, imbedded in the *res publica*, diffused throughout the land; one with the coin of the realm and the flag and the topless wall, the patrician faces in control, the subdued humiliated faces of durance and jeopardy. All one. A system, the correction of which, the reform of which, is as nearly unthinkable as the altering of the majestic, lofty course of the Milky Way; a correction which would bring the most tempestuous shaking of political structures and pinnacles.

In his address before sentencing in Baltimore court, November 1968, Philip made bold to invite all present; judge, prosecutor, bailiffs, church men and women, those inside and outside the court, across the land, to initiate and undergo such changes. To step down. To join us. To join humanity. To join the peacemakers. To cast off their robes, their perquisites, their bejargoned minds, their lethal underhand loyalties.

It was a stunning grace he offered; moreover, the offer was made by a prisoner, in chains, a guarantee that the offer was serious, and costly.

Need I add that he was not taken up? That the judge continued judging (which is to say, misjudging) the prosecutor continued prosecuting (which is to say, making points, creating malefactors). The war continued, the warlike spirit prevailed. And we went on to prison in our turn; in Philip's case, for a substantial portion of his life.

Was the mandate of the gospel obeyed? "Prepare no defense"?

I am proud to say that as far as my understanding goes, it was—and is. We have made mistakes aplenty, as our critics fervently remind us, and rather constantly. Indeed, our mistakes are on public record, as is practically every jot and tittle of our lives. So I feel no pressing call to glory in my infirmities on these pages.

What I am proud of is the consistency that binds the last twenty years in a coherent and even exciting unity. We have never reneged in difficult times on what we promised in rosier times. We have spoken the truth in public, in years when such activity had a bloody price tag attached. When the country was engaged in a mad international hunting party, we refused to ride to the hounds after human pelts and parts. More, we objected to the game, and raised a cry. For being spoil sports in a cannibal time, we paid up. And we continue to pay up; for the game, though costly and foolish and regarded here and there with horror, is by no means abandoned. The hounds of hell are on short traces; they grow voracious for human meat.

Let the record show, we paid up. And continue to do so. In the court of contention and heat and scrambled brains and strangled lives known as the modern world, let the record speak for itself.

A MODEST PROPOSAL TO THE COURT
(Jan. 31, 1977, Alexandria, Virginia)

I would like to open with a supposition whose point will shortly become clear.

Suppose that in a small German town, in 1942, there was brought before a judge a group of accused troublemakers. They had been rounded up by the police at a rather seedy, smoke-ridden, heavily guarded camp near the town. There, went the complaint, they had paraded in death masks, leafletted, shouted sentences about "genocide," refused to move when so ordered. They had even poured over the gates of the camp a "red substance which they declared was their own blood."

The defendants were undoubtedly fractious; they annoyed the court exceedingly. On that hushed air their intemperate voices arose. The camp, they declared, was a vast extermination mill, where children, women, the aged and ill, were routinely slaughtered like cattle in an abattoir, their flesh processed into soap, their bones into buttons, their hair into upholstery, their teeth into pendant ornaments. A use had been found at last for "human life devoid of value." So went their accusation.

The camp commandant took the stand. He was, he declared, all but speechless; such garbled idiocies! The camp, one among many such instruments of the fatherland, was, in fact, performing certain tasks under the immediate supervision of the department of defense. Tasks intimately connected with the security of the people. These dissenters must be mad. He spread his hands.

Thereupon he was questioned by defense counsel. He answered, stern, impeccably polite. He was permitted to reveal exactly—nothing. No detail of the work, production, numbers of workers, wages. No information relative to the camp. Security demanded secrecy in a time of grave national crisis.

Would he comment on this fact? The fallout of peculiarly filthy, acrid smoke, drifting on the town when winds were southwardly.

He would not. National security.

Would he deny in court, under oath, that crimes against humans were being planned or executed in the camp?

The blue eyes of the commandant widened, the eyes of an innocent castaway in a guilty world. National security aside (he declared in ringing tones), I summon my honor, my love for the fatherland, to declare solemnly that no crimes are contemplated or executed under my jurisdiction.

Now to imagine the outcome of all this is no great feat. In high places the vigorous lie always prevails over the bizarre truth. That is how the high and mighty retain both height and might; which is to say, practically speaking, a boot pressed to the neck of the hapless—who thereby learn, among other lessons, the danger of exceeding a befitting modesty.

But what of the judge who vindicates the bully in the boot? His decree invariably goes like this; it is dignum et justum, *moreoever,* aequum et salutare, *that the military rest its gargantuan iron-shod hoof squarely on the jugular vein of humanity.* Dignum, *indeed! Under this august heel, who but a malcontent would fret, since no* foreign *heel can be allowed to threaten this precious body, while our hundred pound iron-bound hoof protects it? Let us, in fine, be grateful for national security, inconvenient as it may be, or throttling to intemperate freedom.*

But imagine for a moment a different judge, another outcome. Imagine! This extraordinary Dachau judge (he is pure fiction) rises from his seat, abruptly halts the proceedings, announces that the commandant, the accused, and himself are to proceed immediately to the camp precincts. He, too, had smelled a mysterious odor on the wind, had pondered within himself; if such a smoke lay on the air, what were the fires like?

Now, the court will agree, our story has taken an absurd turn. What magistrate anywhere in the world, would accept the word of a few deviants against the sworn evidence of a spiffy, punctilious officer? This is unthinkable; our imaginary judge took no one's word about an event conflictingly reported. He was not operating a public relations center for the military, neither was he accepting the hearsay of dissenters. No, he merely said to himself; I can smell, I can see, I will smell this thing out. I will not decide for the military because they are proud and assured, nor for the dissenters because they appear conscientious. I will judge for myself—which is, after all, what a judge is for. I will not be politicized, I will not be awed. I will not, above all, be previous. I will follow my nose.

Let us follow this singular personage, as he rises from the seat of judgment, fervently on the move for simple evidence.

What he found at the camp was indeed monstrous; the smoke led him to the fire, and the fire to that horrid combustible matter, human flesh. He then shouted aloud. His decree and sentence fell like the crack of doom. He was heard. He revealed a crime. He saved lives. He restored a degraded judiciary. He also, beyond doubt, paid for all this.

I wish this morning to press my analogy. Troublemakers are before the court. They recall that on December 9, 1976, Kissinger urged a group of NATO commanders in Europe, in effect; keep your camps open, keep them at the ready. For our camps are open and ready, the ovens are stoked; let's burn them before they burn us.

This is the newest form of that horrid news that has brought us defendants, time and again, to the camp gates. We ask you, judge, do you smell what we smell? Is it true by Nuremberg statute, as well as domestic law, that it is a criminal act to conspire to commit a crime? Is it true that such conspiracy already includes and supposes the crime, that if intent is established, an indictment can proceed?

Come with us to the camp. Judge for yourself. If but one judge would demand the production of evidence of intent, prior to any attack on the U.S., utterly to destroy the cities of Russia and China, if files revealed the construction of weaponry to arm such an intent—what then?

We say—the conspiracy is underway. The weapons are concocted. The plan is well advanced.

We ask then, how you can find us guilty. We by no means ask you to take our word. We ask you to demand evidence, which we claim is in the files of the war department, of a criminal conspiracy against humanity. We claim that the most horrid crime in the history of humanity is being planned there: a conspiracy to Hiroshimize every city of the world, to pulverize and vaporize all flesh and bones, to declare the human adventure a cul-de-sac, history null and void.

Indeed, in the case now before the court, the smoke would lead to the fire, and the fire to combustible flesh. And your discovery of evidence, your judicial protest, would sound like the crack of doom. You would be heard, when we are not heard. You would reveal a great crime. You would save lives. You would also restore a degraded judiciary.

Our proposal does indeed seem modest enough, relative to the proper dignity and function of humans, namely; that doctors heal, that teachers teach, that judges dispense justice.

In practice, however, we know how bad times cut us down, we see with dismay the diminished possibility and performance of officials. Thus, with a certain irony, Florence Nightingale could write from the Crimea in the nineteenth century; "I am not at all certain of what a hospital is for. But I am reasonably sure it is not meant for the spread of disease."

Admirable modesty! And Camus wrote after the Second World War: "We do not seek a world in which murder does not occur. We are grown modest. We seek a world in which murder is not legitimate."

Of one thing we, the defendants, are sure. The Pentagon is planning the nuclear murder of humanity.

Of a second thing, corollary of the first, we are unsure. Whether the proper function of a magistrate is to render murder legitimate. This, I take it, is a question only a magistrate can answer.

Still, though the answer lies with you, we can offer clues as to its direction.

—You give the nod to murder when you mistrust us and trust the camp commanders about the events transpiring at the camp.

—You give the nod to murder, though time and again we bring to you urgent word of a crime in preparation. You ignore our word, you ignore the crime.

—You give the nod to murder when the commanders, time and again, hand us over to you, knowing their enterprise is secure and ours, to say the least, in jeopardy.

—You give the nod to murder by honoring the presumption of American authority: the presumption of their innocence in high crime, and the presumption of our guilt in civil disobedience.

—You give the nod to murder, finally, by sticking to the letter of the law. The letter of this law, quite literally, kills. It will kill you, as it will kill all those who bow to it, countenance it, obey it. It will sweep you into an awesome conspiracy, will add your name to the blueprint of the mad engineers, a blueprint now being drawn up in your judicial district. The blueprint is marked, "Plans for the Last Day."

6. Let Him Who Is Without Sin . . . Be the First to Throw a Stone

(John 8:7)

It is highly unpleasant to the settled conscience to recall that, according to Isaiah and Hosea, the so-called faithful are often found faithless. Those who have entered covenants—marriage, friendship, vows of whatever consequence—are at times discovered *in flagrante delicto.*

Thus, the flavor and irony of John's story. He places the episode of the woman taken in adultery and her accusers in an ancient setting, as old as Jewish memory—a long memory indeed.

In such a setting, the woman, whom art (male art, churchy art) has pictured crouched at the feet of her tormentors, stands up. She becomes a Draconian figure, a Deborah, a Rachel, a warrior, the worrier of infected conscience.

It is Jesus who, as usual, turns the tables. His regal hand flips over; now it is the vindictive and hypocritical who languish in the dust.

The woman is haled before Him. Her partner? There is no partner; it is as though adultery were a solitary sin, a female sin, a sin of the temptress; even a crime in which the male is seduced, raped, violated. As in other cultures and times, the male is invisible; or at least, guiltless. We hear his plaint, an echo from the primordial garden; the woman tempted me, and I ate.

Leave it at that, she is a woman, the burden of sin, which her accusers are pleased to call a crime, falls only to her.

But wait, Jesus has other ideas. They issue from His ironic imagination, which insists here and elsewhere, that reality is other than the law, other than convention or sexual mores. He insists on a fact; the woman had a partner. And not one, but many. Not merely the one who had free access to her bed, and an exit from the law. But more, her partners are also her accusers, who now surround her like animals moving in for a kill.

This is dangerous talk indeed, and will land Him in trouble.

But in what does their sin consist, who accuse this woman with such headlong fervor, as though, indeed in some flagrant sense, she had sinned against them?

Surely, something more is in question than their secret lusts; the point would be frivolous, out of kilter with the dense symbolic and historical sense of John. Nor would such a meaning turn the tables on them; it would merely shuffle cards in the same deck. Rather it seems as though the Lord passes, with disdain and speed, out of their moral orbit, into His own, draws them along in spite of themselves; (they, after all, having started the unsavory proceeding). And that orbit, as John knows so well, is the imagination of Jesus; His skill at grasping the deep motor drives of men, at riding them to their sources, at sweeping away prevarication and coverup, especially when these walk abroad in the self-mocking charade of religion and law.

A dangerous game, this turning of tables. The law, and religion so understood, so shored up, so protected, so hand in hand with the forces of this world, with the demonic structures of history—the arrangement is a very gorgon of self-interest and skilled survival. Not for nothing have church and state joined hands; the mutuality of interests, defense, protection, are very nearly impermeable. Let this rabbi take warning. . . .

Nevertheless, He declares their sin; it is murder, vindictiveness, cruelty. He names it: names it in silence, in seemingly ignoring them, in turning aside, idly, as though to scribble meaninglessly in the dust, as though this hanging jury were unworthy of serious attention. They persist, they push matters. He must be reminded, such punishment as they seek is sanctioned by law. This is the sinister fact, the dilemma they are pushing at Him, an indictment is signed and sealed in their code. Moses allows legitimate capital force against this sinner, this female.

The law is on their side. They drag the criminal before Him, in a drama of charged passion. They mean to have Him on the horns; the woman is by no means their sole prey. "In the law, Moses commanded us to stone such [women]. What do you say?"

The vindictiveness of the scene, its malice, its moral squalor, are overwhelming. We sense, as Christ did, the odor of their turpitude. It swirls about them, emanates from them, a stench of death. How they hate the good that would impede and judge—not her, but themselves! So they purpose to include Him in the deadly swath of the law; He is its target, she merely its occasion. For if He consents to the woman's death, He publicly repudiates His message of mercy, compassion. And if He objects to their design, then the circle of death widens to include Him, her self-declared accomplice.

To note that in such a crisis, Jesus stands at the woman's side, determined to save her, this is indeed worthy of awe and pondering. As on other occasions, He stands with the outcast Samaritan woman at the well, the lepers, the condemned tax collectors, the rag-tag elements of street, market, hovel. This is godlike activity; we are astonished and delighted (or perhaps frightened, dismayed). Such conduct, we think, may measure the distance separating us from the godlike One—as well as from our own humanity. But at least the distance is measurable, and its measure is taken here, and the gap closed for a moment. One among us has closed it. And His name is God, and God with us.

Still, I sense a deeper plea here than the saving of the woman. The scene includes Jesus as codefendant. In succoring the woman, in appearing as her spontaneous advocate, in breaking through the vicious circle of the law, Jesus is also pleading His own cause.

Indeed, His exemplary action comes home in just this way: to Himself. It may be a Platonic truth I am suggesting, but it is truer than any school of wisdom. If He breaks bread, it is not only bread that is broken; it is His own body. So with the cup He passes; it is the gift of life, His own. These sublime and exalted actions are a clue to much else in Him (and in us). They close the gap which sin has opened, which lies across our spirit, a wound unhealed; the act without soul, the speech cheap and redundant, the spirit inarticulate, twisted. (If we break bread and pass a cup, are these not sour and stale, and speak for little of self-giving, self-healing?)

But if there were not in Him something of the woman and her plight in this world, surrounded as she is by the ravenous and vengeful, He and she suspect, endangered—could He have responded as He did, promptly, with imagination, almost without effort, a discharge of sure conscience, scoring the bull's eye of truth?

There is a simpatico deep as all compassion, the compassion of the universe itself for its tender and vulnerable members, the compassion of the Lord of the Vow. It saves, it alone saves. Neither Pharaoh nor his arms or horsemen. . . . But such love as this unveils to our gaze the heart of the one who would succor and save. And we are graced at the sight.

He knew the danger implicit in standing with her. And He placed Himself, in full deliberation, in her circle. Now the advocate and defendant are one, surrounded, endangered, all but convicted. He is collusive to her crime, in resisting its due outcome.

In fighting for her, He fights for Himself. His altruism includes a necessary and legitimate self-interest. Even God, taking sides as He does, must defend Himself. And to the death, because death would prevail at all cost (we sense here their last ditch will), would count as its greatest triumph the death of God.

Far from mere palaver, Jesus advances proceedings. He proposes a delicious Zen twist: the dilemma they cast at Him is thrown back. "Let him who is without sin among you be the first to throw a stone."

Now matters rest in their hands. Can one among them be found who is sinless, who has not broken promises, broken vows, broken trust with the God who calls for mercy? And supposing the presence of such a one, could he bear to collaborate in the proceedings which, as they know (Jesus has instructed them remorselessly) are no act of justice, but plain vengeance? Presuming the presence of an unassailable holy one among them, a very hammer of God, can such a one approve the execution of the woman? And so doing, can he remain, in his own estimate, sinless?

Whether such a one stood among the self-appointed just, we are not told. Jesus leaves matters where they stand, in stalemate. We are told only that they slink away, one after the other, to the last—a unanimity of restraint rarely found in the godly.

And He is left alone with the woman (which is to say, from another point of view, with His own soul). He has indeed won her case. But must one not add the dolorous fact, that He is closer to losing His own? She is vindicated. But for Himself, He has won no more than a respite, a stay of execution.

The woman is dismissed with infinite gentleness, the most delicate of reproofs. And He turns away, and enters, we may think, more deeply into Himself and His fate.

My mind reverts to the theme of covenant and betrayal, the sin of the accusers. Presumably, the woman had been seized, or effectively denounced by witnesses, in violation of a vow—her's or another's. But, as Jesus insists, her judges had violated a far greater trust than that of the flesh. They are the disruptors and destroyers of mercy in the world, they would stop the divine activity in its tracks, seal up the sources of vision. They push the justice of men, evil and tawdry substitute for the mercy of God. . . .

When all is said, the message Jesus offers is an extremely simple one. One sentence goes to the heart of the matter (the matter of the nation state, the matter of the church, of the citizen and believer). Thou shalt not betray. It is uttered to the woman as well as to her accusers and thwarted killers.

Ironically, the drama reaches its highest moment in the God who does not betray. He stands majestic, immoveable, at the opposite pole from those whose chief skill is betrayal, whose lives are built on the breaking of promises, who break bones in the name of justice, or a code, of law and order. Standing there, His scorn rains down, the contempt of the truly human toward the merely contemptible.

Then He simply forgives, wipes the account clean. He takes the woman to heart; His own complement.

What relief is offered by this scene, its high drama, its quietly perfect diminuendo! Such vignettes, lowly and hidden as they are, open a moral world to our eyes, welcome a dawn. How else indeed, supposing the stupendous truth of the Incarnation of God, does one expect God to treat with the lonely and unacceptable, the "sinners" created by the vicious and virtuous?

A confession is called for here. Today the church is as uneasy and guilt-ridden as the circle of accusers, before the community of women. Women are regarded in the church, despite the manifest will of Christ, as those "taken in adultery": they are suspect, under judgment from birth, denied access to altar and pulpit, consigned to lowest places—pariahs whose only crime is their biology.

To confess that such malign arrangements are unworthy of the church of Christ is to convey little of the rage and confusion of spirit that must afflict thoughtful Christians. The battle for womens' rights continues in a disoriented and violent society, and the church throws up its own barricades, settles in for an indefinite siege. And the justifying rhetoric, offered straight-faced and with due solemnity, defies reason and scripture alike.

Let us say only that such talk condemns itself in the act. And let us mourn that such "theological reasoning" serves only to perpetuate the rule of unreason.

Meantime, the church's life is poisoned at its source. Let me speak for myself and a few priest friends. We are betrayed in the betrayal of women, shunted into an indefensible position; a bad faith so terrible as to taint the sacraments we offer the faithful.

We stand at the altar, no longer the free ministers of the gift of Christ, no longer priests of a church from which all pollution of class and sex and color and politics has been purified at one great stroke. Purified? We are now rigidly classified ourselves, divided in soul, subject to rightful derision, made to justify (at last by silence) indefensible marching orders.

In spite of all, we cannot deceive ourselves. The church will win no hearing on the moral issues cast up by the chaos of modern life, as long as the women of the church stand outside—or stand accused.

No deceiving ourselves. It is those who condemn without cause, whose language is corrupted by self-serving casuistry, by a determination to preserve an indefensible status quo—it is these who stand under judgment.

Not the women.

Let the mighty fear mightily. For the soul of Christ is, in large and luminous part, the soul of a woman. And Christ is God. A woman shall judge them.

7. Lazarus, Come Forth

(John 11:43)

In a world given over to death, I ask myself, What is my expectation of Christ?

This week a child died in the cancer ward, after two years in our midst. He lay there comatose, a sublime, vegetating beauty, a bud never to flower. Time, after time, I saw his eyelids flutter;

one eye unfocused, the other came to rest on me. It was as though he reposed or whirled in an orbit out of this world. But he never once spoke; his hands, their fingers bent back in spasm, were helpless evidence of his sleeping soul. So he lived, and so died.

Like all who visited the ward, I was shaken to the core by his plight. A kind of wary silence took over, I held his hand, stroked his face, breathed a prayer and departed. What was there to say—to him, to myself? Thought lay too deep for tears.

What is my expectation of Christ?

I never prayed for a miracle. I let the child go. Not knowing what else to do. Not being in command of the universe, or of a single life, including my own.

At the same time, I want to separate such reflections from any indifference or blunting of mind. I hope my love for the child stands clear. Still, letting him go even as I took him to heart, the question remains: What do I expect of Christ?

Expectation, hope. The future, the Coming. Flat endurance, event. These words circle about in my brain.

Let me think of the unlikeliest event conceivable in this world. First, a tragedy, a loss, let us say the death of a dear one. Shocking, unexpected. Shortly thereafter, friends stand grieving at an open grave.

So far, so bad, an event we can admit as a possibility for anyone in the world, including one's self.

Suddenly, this scene of mute grief is brought to a halt, invaded, confronted. Someone is in the midst of the mourners, Someone who is not mourning. The tears, the vertigo, the emotional welter of death, halt in midair. Someone stands there. He is also a friend, but He is no mourner.

Indeed, He commands attention, shockingly, with power. Lazarus, come forth.

We are fascinated, horrified even, attention wildly divided. The mouth of the grave, the face of the living?

Then the unthinkable occurs. A dead man stands in our midst, living.

But, what of us today? Who will never stand at such a scene, take it in? That scene of the newly risen?

We commonly judge that we will have to deal only with death; and that, we say, is quite enough. Never in this world will we witness death undone, the once dead standing in our midst, and we grown wild, beside ourselves with joy.

Never. And yet I think, it is against such an event as this, that our expectation of Christ (which is also our expectation of ourselves) must be measured. The unlikeliest event in the world. The event we will never see with mortal eyes. The event we only hear of, the one we must take on the word of others and they removed from us by nearly infinite vistas, centuries. An event we must take on the word of one who purportedly brought such a thing to pass: "Take it from me; I did this thing."

Never did I pray that the child might be healed. Such a prayer seemed presumptuous. I never allowed myself the hope that the child would stand again, walk among us, healthy and restored. Letting the child go, letting go his hand, my hope for him. Standing in spirit at his grave. And I must report sorrowfully that I was right, the child died. I never witnessed a Lazarus moment.

The child died in the course of nature; as they say with a sigh, this is the way the world goes. No intervention. No reversal of the sad and slow tread, the pall bearers, the shuffle and weeping of the family, the stupefied grief of those (myself included) who cannot understand, who only half yield the child up (only half yield ourselves up?).

Take this likely event of the child's death, the likeliest event in the world. And consider that in all the centuries since Lazarus, there has been no such unlikely intervention. People die, the young and innocent, the aged and tired. Death by violence, by malice, by misadventure, death wholesale, death one-by-one, death by genocide, by war, by roadside slaughter. And no intervention, not one. No Lazarus walks toward us.

Let me take this fact and omnipresence and pressing urgency and claimant death, and consider what is at hand for us. The strong likelihood is that, in our lifetime, death will so prevail as to call a halt, not to this or that life, nor even to a multitude, through some war, some monstrous fault or failure in nature, some act of wanton terror. Nothing so small, so paltry. The area now ceded to death being the round of the earth itself, and all inhabitants, and finally, all living beings.

This is what draws near, not death as natural outcome, death as eventuality, death the "futurable," death taken more or less seriously, taken into account or no, well or badly prepared for, condemned or welcomed.

Everything in our history points to one dolorous conclusion: the eventual or prompt discharge of nuclear weapons. Indeed, history is appallingly consistent with this outcome. No weapon, once conceived, ever rotted or rusted unused. No weapon, once created, failed to create an enemy. No enemy so created failed to duplicate the weapon, and to improve on it. No weapons systems since gunpowder, failed to be used in actual warfare. And no war, so provoked, ever once produced peace. The prophet Jeremiah puts the vicious cycle of death in a sentence: "Out of peace, war, out of war, more war: out of war never once peace."

All this is sobering enough. Still, in the past we could always comfort ourselves after the event, the horror. For we still had time, time to learn, time to repair, rebuild, time even to make a precarious peace.

What we failed to realize was this: It was the weapons that gave us time, and no wisdom of ours. This is a deep and bitter understanding; we were fatally slow in coming to it, because while we knew our weapons well (had we not, after all, created them?), we were fatally retarded in self-knowledge. It was the weapons that gave us time. They were vile and horrid, but they were merciful too, in measure: they knew limits. They were applied, discharged in limited wars, they fulfilled the limiting prophecies of Revelation; one fourth of the earth destroyed, one-third of the streams polluted, a certain limited number of humans killed.

Still, the mercy of the weapons was no measure of our own. They would kill only one, or a few, or many, or a multitude, or bring down a city (even in their so-called conventional phase, let alone their nuclear phase). Thus, they placed limits on us. But we must understand (the Bible understands)—we, our merciless will, our malice, always tended toward more and more violence, total destruction, the end phase of life. We were hot after weapons that would make Hitler's blitzkrieg look like the arsenal of a back street thug.

The Bible teaches in many places, warns, illustrates, denounces, illumines this bitter truth: the violence of humans is in essence genocidal, mass suicidal. War is not itself until it is total war, laying claim to the total person, the human family in toto, universal life. Such a will, in our lifetime, creates weapons to match its madness; and for once, the weapons are equal to the will. They are merciless as ourselves, they at length resemble us, our alter ego. War has thus become the ultimate anti-Christ, the obscene god of death, condemning all life to capital punishment.

Now, we have death, the "final solution" to what has become, in all mad sobriety, a universal problem, the problem of life itself. Whether life is, as they say, worth living, whether the living regard life (their lives, all lives) as precious or cheap, a phenomenon of merely relative interest or of consummate value, a peak, a gift irreplaceable—or a burden, a night sweat, a nuisance.

We are not standing in spirit today at this or that grave. However deeply we have tasted the bitterness of death, we must understand that something altogether unheard of, a tragedy unparalleled, a horror that beggars description, is growing ever more likely. The world itself is in danger of being plowed open, from a place of teeming life to a cosmic grave. The world itself is grown Lazarine, the human race is rolled in a shroud.

And what now? What is our expectation of Christ? The above likelihood being admitted, as cold fact and strong probability, dallied with by straight faces and purportedly sane minds, the means of the monstrous crime being created day after day, the ideology to justify the crime being also prepared, heated up, the president rattling the nuclear sword, the congress rising to its feet with a roar, the people transfixed or assenting or merely perplexed, but in nearly every instance unable or unwilling to resist. . . .

What now? What is our expectation of Christ? Has the likelihood of universal death so abused our sense of the sacred (of the truly human) that we now conclude that Christ, too, is transfixed or traumatized or plain helpless—but in any case, unable or unwilling to act?

For my own part, I cannot separate His activity in the world from my own. I see Him in the gospel and the Eucharist, but also in the faithful—in the mirror of my own mind and the work of my hands.

To pray for His intervention is to imply my own. I do not know of another way of regarding our impasse, or a possible breakthrough. This is why I am arrested again and again, and will never give up. This is why, as I write this, my friends and family are in jail, or in the courts, or are so arranging their lives as to increase such a likelihood. We believe that every office and charism granted us over the years—priest, teacher, writer, friend of the dying, spouse, parent—all and each of these verified, must test their will against our expectation of Christ in the world.

I believe further, that it is not the method of God to intervene in events, not miraculously. This is the evidence I gather from the Bible, as from those who live with their eyes open. Genuine hope turns our eyes in another direction than the miraculous. Let us say—hope turns our eyes in the direction of modest possibilities. Which, being faithfully pursued and clung to, make death bearable and grant courage to the living.

So believing, I deny to the politicians, the researchers, the generals, their way in the world. They will not prevail. My faith in Christ and my faith in my friends allows me to say this. The word of the death dealers is not the last word about our fate; other hands than theirs are in command of life and death.

The child, that dear friend who could never name me as his friend, is dead. But I will see him again, and hear him utter a word his poor lips could not form in this world. And for his green memory, and for the sake of all children, our most endangered species, I will keep faith.

8. Compel Them to Come In

(Luke 14:23 KJV)

This is a story about me.

I am one of those latecomers, who would never have come to the table at all but for one dim chance and hope. Would never have sat there, since first of all, I was not on the original list of invited guests. Nor am I one of the "poor and crippled and blind and lame" who must have been, in Christ's time as in ours, numerous beyond number, and would leave small room for others. And yet there was room, room for me.

Who then am I?

I try to imagine who I am in the world.

One way of doing so is to imagine who I am in the imagination of Jesus.

Somewhere in this story, I am convinced, He has imagined me.

I was not originally invited, nor am I one of those named in the catalogue of ills and misfortunes that assures one of an engraved invitation to the feast.

Still, all is not lost. Following on these, a third invitation is issued. And it includes me, at last.

"Go out into the highways and hedges, and compel them to come in" (14:23 KJV). It is not said who they are. It is implied, however, who they are not. Not, in the first place, those with worldly connections, a glittering future, ample choices, a good sensible command of power and money and the goods of the earth. Not those who, under threat of a deluge, as we are told in Genesis, maintain a hideous normalcy, who "marry and give in marriage." Not the normal people, the good worldly hard-nosed people, those with an eye to the main chance. Not those with, as they say, clear priorities, a piece of hot real estate, spanking spans of oxen, and (in the same catalogue of havings and holdings, of real estate and unreal cupidity)—a wife. And what, after all, is a mere dinner compared with this enlightened wheeling and dealing, this frenetic, cold-eyed commerce? RSVP? Thank you, but no thank you.

Then the second wave, the "unfortunate ones." They hobble and clamber and grope their way to the table, one helping the other, another impeding a third, in the race for seats and a free meal in the big house on the hill. And I am not among those.

Where then?

"Go out into the highways and hedges, and compel them to come in." Not many clues as to who these, so to speak, last-ditch guests are. Except, by implication, a clue as to who they are not. Neither the fortunate, nor (at least as previously enumerated), the unfortunate.

Who then? Who is it that walks the highways, or hitchhikes on them? And what sort of creature hangs out in hedgerows?

I like first of all, the anonymity of the image. It seems large enough to include almost anyone with two feet under him, with a nose to the winds coming over the horizon. A hobo? A mental patient? A beat? A pilgrim? A castoff? A fugitive?

In any case, someone on the move. . . .

We were farm people in upstate New York. My father used to refer wryly to us six boys as *depression babies*. We had ten acres of clay, a few livestock, and a deep reserve of stubbornness. So we made it through some of the leanest seasons on record since the Egyptians' hoarded wheat.

One day, there arrived at our kitchen door a portent the likes of whom a child's eyes are seldom granted to behold. This poor, wild-eyed, ragged creature! A figure out of *Les Miserables;* he had undoubtedly passed nights and days in the swamps nearby; in face and crouch and growl, he was like a ravenous wolf.

In the house were my mother and two small children, Philip and myself. She opened the door (I never forgot the scene), the two of us sprats peering out from her skirts. And without missing a beat (but did her heart miss a beat?), she waved this inarticulate bag of bones into her house.

No questions asked. Something quite typical of her; what the theologians call "unconditional love."

Love with an edge. She laid a cloth and began to prepare a meal: a dozen eggs and trimmings, fresh bread and butter, coffee snarling from the pot. The wolf at the door was wolfish at table. Without a word, he polished off everything within reach. He was silent as a stone, my mother silently came and went, serving him. Then, in the pantry, she worked away preparing sandwiches and fruit for him to take along.

Which he did, departing, mumbling something incomprehensible in his beard, maybe a word of thanks.

And within ten minutes, lo! A carload of state troopers swarmed in the yard, yelling word of an escaped convict in the area. And my mother calm and usual in manner, standing between the listening children, answered: Yes, someone of that description had been in her home, and yes she had fed him, and yes he had gone off in that (and she pointed up the road) direction. And they racing off like the hounds of hell on the spoor of our poor guest.

And I, age five, knowing something instinctively. That she had pointed the pursuers in exactly the wrong direction. Knowing, too, as children will, that she could act in no different wise, since everything of her life, her aura, her courage, born of poverty and crushing labor and the bearing and raising of six children, everything was predictable, like a healing shadow cast ahead of her at evening. The shadow of one who invariably shelters the victim. And who, having fed a fugitive at her table in exactly the way she would feed her family at the same table, refusing to pass food out at the door, as to a hungry animal, but inviting him in from highway and hedge, and spreading the cloth—after this spontaneous, congruous conduct, by no means would she cap her good act by surrendering so sorry a creature into the hands of police.

Bravo, dear, dead lady, ineradicable example! You showed two little children a way, without ever pausing to recollect that they would remember such an hour, such a woman, the event stamped on them like a birthmark, to their dying day. . . .

I, too, have been a fugitive for months, pursued by a great squad (we only learned much later how numerous) of federal hounds on loose traces. And found loyal and dependable friends at every turn of what was indeed a treacherous and crooked road. And was, in a true sense, "compelled" again and again "to come in," was fed and harbored; a criminal, one from "the highways and hedges."

You have to go there to know the way there. You have to be rejected and outcast to taste the sweetness of being invited in.

Or, as my mother used to say, putting the matter differently, "You have to know hunger, to know how to spread a table."

9. Flee

(Matthew 24:16)

There is a disturbing consonance between the long discourse of Jesus in Matthew on the final days (chap. 24) and the Babylon passage in Revelation (chap. 18). It is as though Jesus, sensing that His time had come, sensed also that His fate was joined irrevocably to the fate of others. Not only He was going under, gods do not die alone. Their fate convulses community and nature; their death opens a fault in the earth.

When you see the "abomination of desolation" spoken of by the prophet Daniel, standing in the holy place, "let those who are in Judea flee to the mountains." The admonition signals a final clash between the holy and the demonic. And in Revelation, under the stress of a different crisis, a parallel action is urged. "Come out of here [Babylon], my people, lest you take part in her sins, lest you share in her plagues; for her sins are heaped high as heaven, and God has remembered her iniquities."

In Revelation, certain events precipitate the advice to "flee." The Lord refers to a mysterious pollution of the temple, foreseen by the prophet Daniel, an idol set up in the holy place. And in Revelation, sins and plagues seeded by the empire threaten the integrity, even the existence, of the faithful community.

There are perhaps two ways of reacting to such nightmares. The question naturally arises: Do such events as are pointed to come to pass, do the symbols "abomination of desolation" and "sins and plagues" really signal historical moments verified then and now?—do the prophecies issue in events, polluting and repressive laws, wars, blasphemies, the ousting of God from His temple?

Or are such unsettling images to be taken as mere seismic shifts, shadowy reminders of evil in the world, warnings of dangers that always remain at distance, remote evils, a darkness that invades without quenching the light of holiness?

Answers, of course, vary wondrously. There are Christians who panic at every event, wave Bibles about, coerce and shout of damnation and hellfire. They are commonly referred to as "fundamentalists," a term overlong perhaps to denote a slippage of moorings, loss of nerve, fascination with misfortune, as though God's highest activity were to foment catastrophe in nature and among His people.

But there is another way of regarding the apocalyptic and surreal passages of scripture. To certain academics, almost any scriptural truth is regarded as grist for mere mortician skills. A nightmare, a disaster, moral collapse, warning or foreboding of these—words, words are the point! Verify the word, codify it, explain its historical setting, its genesis in the cultural matrix, its influence on those times . . . Scripture is no more than a dead letter; and this even when its words are dead serious, direly urgent, words of fury, indignation, reproach, retribution.

To the fundamentalist, the Bible is a club with which to beat the underbrush of the world, to scare up a prey: sinners, backsliders, nonbelievers, the unwary and unwashed. To some academics, the word of God is literally weightless. It comes to ground nowhere in this world, nowhere in time—with the exception, of course, of its meaning to the generation that produced it. But Revelation or Matthew, speaking directly to our situation, our political impasse? Absurd. No contemporary horror or crime could cause the word to start to life, to become incendiary, dangerous, to say here and now: "judgment is here and now."

I think of the fundamentalist as a contracted conscience, scripture creating a meticulously petty mind, every contingency covered; the Bible is a set of rules, a flat-out handbook of divine invention and intervention.

And the academic conscience is infinitely expandable; the Bible is an entirely apolitical treatise, certainly great and noble literature, but an Olympian word, at a distance; by no means a call to political responsibility, or a trump of judgment sounding against crimes of high power.

If I were forced to choose (and may God grant that the issue never arise, it is a choice among spikes and barbed quills), I would lean, given the times we must cope with, toward the fundamentalist. I write "lean toward" with some deliberation. I believe that detached scholarship is a greater violation of the hope of God, the divine passion to be heard and rightly understood, the truth entrusted to the hands of the intelligent and privileged. A greater violation than the stretched passion of the clumsy and ignorant, their passion to know, to be assured, comforted, strengthened by God. A strange faith indeed, yelling incontinently in one's ears in public places! But still a faith, a sense of tragedy impending, a will to walk the world step by step with eyes open, in pilgrim combat.

I understand this excess and its failures far better than I understand the betrayal of the academic, whose method makes twentieth-century dead sea scrolls of the living word.

Indeed, to such minds, does that word come down in judgment anywhere in our lifetime? Does it penetrate the political darkness, the military strongholds, whose strongest

hold is precisely our darkened souls? Does that word speak in
the horrific silence of Pentagon corridors at midnight, when
the ghosts walk, the ghosts of humans, the ghosts of ourselves,
condemned to death in mad decisions contrived in such places?

I write these words at a prestigious seminary in California, a
clotting of minds and books and youth and prestige and
purported scriptural savvy. Some of us have been appalled at
recent government events, heavy clouds scudding the sky and
darkening the noon; the thunder and veiled lightnings of
nuclear intervention, the inhuman dragnet of the draft. Some
of us, I say. For many others, it is theological business as usual,
even while the world shudders with premonitions of disaster
and the heart fails in its course. Theology as usual: the
conscience as infinitely expandable, a gas filling a void with its
own soporific. More than one renowned divine has been heard
to mutter at the "unseemly intrusions of politics into theology."

So be it. On Ash Wednesday we urged a moratorium on
classes, a vigil, prayer, a teach-in, a march, and a nonviolent
sit-in at the offices of the university officials nearby. For it
seems to us beyond doubt that they are conspiring in high
crime, through aiding the development of nuclear weaponry
at Livermore and Los Alamos death factories.

The texts of Matthew and Revelation urge the faithful to
flee. The actions we engage in, whether legal or outside the
law, are our way of fleeing the abomination, the crime. We
choose, as nuclear apocalypse nears, to contract our conscience, to concentrate its light on a sin that heaps darkness
upon darkness.

We have had enough of weightless scholarship. It floated
above our heads during the Vietnam years, so nearly out of
sight as to be all but invisible to the searching mind, the
conscientious heart.

A kind of absurd consistency here. First Vietnam, now the
nukes. And theology sails regally on, a doomed voyage; good
housekeeping in a madhouse. Neglecting, ignoring the true

intent of its study; the searching of scripture and a tradition of faith to lay the sword of God's judgment against human folly.

Flee the crime.

I ponder this command. There are refugees, hostages, prisoners of conscience everywhere in the world, their numbers multiplied beyond counting. Refugees fleeing crimes, war, disruption of lives. Hostages, captives of violent regimes, women and men paying the price of their service to imperial malpractice. And prisoners in every pocket of the globe, dying in gulags and ghettoes, haled before kangaroo courts, under torture and duress of every kind.

These are the ones to attend to, one eye on our text.

Meantime, what are we to do, who are at large (though ourselves hostages to nuclear terror)?

The question arose time and again during the Vietnam years. It will never cease to arise in our lifetime. To me, the question gives shape and form, even coherence, to life itself. What indeed are we to do with our lives in such mad times?

I conjure up the faces of seminarians, the wary and venturesome, the thoughtful and immature, the newborn and well-tested. A question in every eye: How are we to live?

To them, I said again and again: "the future will be different if we make the present different."

Bonhoeffer's formula: "to live for the coming generation," makes sense only if we are setting about the task of the present generation. There will be no sane or peaceable future unless we are creating here and now a sane and peaceable present; in the very jaws of Leviathan.

10. Go, Teach

(Matthew 28:19, 20 NEB)

May I confess at the start to an inordinate love for teaching? Whether this may imply the high voice of altruism or the low voice of ego has never detained me. What I love is the interplay, subtle and varied as a fugue, minds in clash and consonance, the teacher learning and the students showing their mettle, the light of the mind turning the air incandescent.

Indeed, who is not a teacher? Who is not teachable? What discipline worth the effort does not dissolve the walls of classrooms, opening the soul to the human predicament, the height and breadth of the universe, which is our own true measure?

On exiting from prison in 1972 I made the following resolve: I would not accept a teaching stint for more than one semester; at most (and rarely) for one year.

Further, it would be understood as a condition of employment that I was free to terminate or interrupt the class schedule for the sake of civil disobedience and its consequence. Also that I would favor, in case of two offers of employ, one that brought me among prisoners, the poor, or people in like predicaments.

I have held to the agreement. And so far as may be said of any work in a world such as ours, the arrangement has served me, and others, well.

Certain invariables may be of interest. Academic officials invariably have shown a tight smile at my arrival on their acres, their joy is at times positively incontinent at my departure. The sentiments, may I add, are mutual, and satisfactory.

My salary is the modest equivalent of third world pay; enough for rent and chitlings. I am become, in fact, one of those hewers of wood and bearers of water in the employ of endowed chairs, those who dispense from plush offices, bureaucratic platitudes. And all this, inequitable as may be, is, to put things inelegantly, OK with me.

A classroom is where you find it. In 1970 I voyaged from Cornell, where I had taught and ministered, to Danbury Prison, a slot below the Ivy League, so to speak. I felt, nonetheless, a certain delightful rightness in the move. One had, of course, to swallow the (considerable) differences between the two geographies, the civil and academic statuses implied. So be it, I said to my soul, swallow! I was shortly to discover another class, in more senses than one. It was a kind of dark side of the moon; the subjects were despair, anger, violence, broken lives, racism, macho and punk, suffocation of spirit. Quite an education for the teacher.

And, given the times, given the hyphenated horror Nixon-Mitchell-Hoover, the prison setting, the priest as prisoner-teacher, all had a piquant rightness.

We organized classes, Philip and I, got books in, and started. It was clear that some prisoners wanted desperately to flex their minds. Most had known little or no such discipline in their prior lives. There was even excitement in the air; generated in part, no doubt, by the spectacle of two priests in castoff khaki, stuck, making the best of things for the duration of durance vile.

So it went.

And so it goes. As I set down these random memories in the California sunshine, the clash of Carter's nuclear blade shocks the ear, the Soviets invade, we recoil, the hostages sit on ice in Iran. Here some two hundred seminary sprouts break ground. They and I prepare to march again, this time to the University prexy's office. To present letters of petition that he and his advisers cut off the University connection with the notorious Livermore and Los Alamos Laboratories, where every death egg since Nuclear Year One has brooded and hatched.

We will not succeed, that much is clear. And we will not give up; that is at least equally clear.

That these plans are the necessary and natural consequence of scriptural education (a truth that seems to me self-evident as this morning's brilliant sunrise) is by no means evident among the seminary faculties. Quite the contrary. Such activity, the passage from classroom to street, from theory to the heart of conflict; from, as they say, truth to praxis, this is regarded severally as bizarre, deviant, pointless, disruptive. Or perhaps more commonly, as a matter that holds not the slightest interest for theological minds. The Jesuit faculty, which welcomed me with a mix of wariness and reluctance, keeps that look alive. What can he possibly be up to now?

I am bemused, not at all set back. One retains certain convictions about teaching, amid the beetling brows of academe, secular or theological, upon whom the skies might indeed fall without their turning a learned hair.

I reflect that every campus is like every other campus; get beyond the rhetoric, and the differences go up in smoke. Let public or political or peacemaking responsibilities be broached, and Cornell is one with the Jesuits. Both are, by and large, with a different vocabulary, secularized in conscience and community. To each, the facts of life today—whether they speak of wars, military draft, nuclear horrors, the complicity of institutions with the warmaking corporations and national state—these are no more than shadows on cave walls.

The cave, for all that it offers only semblances and mockups of spiritual reality, has something to commend it; walls and roof are intact. And its fires do more than cast shadows and silhouettes and dreams; the fires also heat bodies and cook food. No energy crisis in the cave, no theological crisis either.

I do not know what brand of religion all this might be named. Any more than I could define the brand of political understanding peddled in years past by the pampered and tenured darlings of Cornell. But perhaps the question is not merely moot but beside the point, since never have these minds met mine in communal understanding about America or Christianity. And one had best leave the discussion there, except to note how wonderfully, even awesomely, once-exalted visions conspire to bring us to ground.

Let me continue in a more promising vein.

Something like this: Who are teachable today?

I dread romanticizing events or experience. No great aura surrounds our lives. One step, then another. If we are lucky, we are never quite stalled; something in us keeps trying the world for size, for comfort, for questions; something, for want of a word, we name—hope. There are friends, their ups and downs, glooms and yells, and our own. And in midst of all, confronting and shaming and meeting our eyes, are those with little or no stake in power, ego, money, sexual hype, the pseudo revolutions which end up digging us larger and deeper graves.

I am trying to describe months I have spent teaching among the urban poor. They did me great, even incalculable, service. They made me reflective, they strengthened my will to resist a system that tolerated (better, created) such horrors as the South Bronx. I would return from these classes in a very stupor of admiration at the skills, survival, good spirit, "dynamism of common natural power" shown there (to use Paul Goodman's phrase).

Or I think of one or another cancer patient at St. Rose's Home. I remember most vividly those whose life took out no insurance on damnation, those who, far back, before their deaths, refused the sops of the culture. And who, at the end, sail out with the tides, owing nothing, conceding nothing to America.

Or I recall elsewhere in more conventional settings (rarely), a face in a crowded classroom, a face capable of silence, a face of inwardness, taking one, so to speak, at face value.

If you wish to convey a vision, you do not shout it into a prevailing wind. Nor do you waste it against a stone wall, or expound it on an animal farm, or among the dead. There is a porous quality, a permeable soul required, if seed is to land and take root. For it is so small a seed, all but a dust, a pollen on the air, it dies, it is blown about or brushed aside by heedless hands.

Who is teachable today? "Connatural" I believe is the lovely word. The soul is connatural with the truth.

But not always and everywhere. Americans, including those who call themselves American Christians, are not invariably connatural with the truth, the vision. They (we) are commonly, in fact, at great odds with it. The national life, in marketplace or churches, builds itself up like a wall of coral; dense, mortised, massive, it teeters like the wall described by Isaiah, it falls a dead weight.

Skill without vision, the academic morass. Professionalism gutted of the will to serve. Ivory towers shored up with shady grants and privileges. "Value-free" research, indentured to the warmaking government. The university as whore, the seminary as fatuous handmaid to a dying culture. . . .

I came on another translation of the command of Jesus, "Go, . . . and teach." It went: "Go, make disciples." I like this, as long as the understanding is something like: Go, speak the truth. Or, Go, vindicate life. Or, Go, resist death.

I like also Gandhi's statement, "Rather than creating disciples" he declared, "I seek opposite numbers." Is not this to our purpose, that we become, now or in the future, a mature community of enlightened spirits who are willing, not only to hear and speak the truth, but to pay up?

The times are dark, and grow darker. No one need be told. We are ignorant as sticks and stones, public folly seizes on public apathy, the sleepers pass from sleep to death. Teaching is a disheartening business; it seems as though the wellsprings are poisoned, as though an ancient wisdom has fled elsewhere. We long to offer a coherent body of truth, not only to bespeak our predicament, but to heal it. Our tongues stutter before the horrid burden we live under; all we can utter like the deep groan of Jeremiah, is something like: "Thou shalt not kill."

I asked myself the question: "Who is teachable today"? A friend, dying of cancer, wrote me the following. (I arrange the words in broken lines because they seem to me the purest poetry):

> I am not outside the malaise
> My happiness consists in having conquered the malaise
> while living
> in the center of it
> The malaise is the fear
> that humans may be after all
> only a blighted species
> unfit as any animal
> a sport in the house of nature
> and fated to bring all down in ruin
> Against this
> I call up the faces of my loved ones
> and refuse to give them up to death
> It is because I have won in this fight
> that I am happy.

III

A Dialogue with My Soul on What I Take to Be the Heart of the Matter

I: The topic, I believe, is something like "sacrificial love." I take it that this is where you part company with the world?

Soul: I think so. As long as you understand the "world," not as some closed system or astrodome, we out here, they in there.

I: Then how should I understand the world?

Soul: Out here *and* in here. Call it pollution. Call it possession, as the Bible does. Or technique, in the sense of norms or values that stake out their own turf, a turf as wide as the world. And call it "mine"! And dare God to invade it.

I: Now, you've given it all away. You've just defined Marxism, "staking off this world for its turf." More, Marxists have died for their beliefs, shown what you call sacrificial love—done it at least as grandly and nobly as the Christians. Nor do I want to bring up here an unpleasant Christian skill: coming in late for an action, and then laying claim to the benefits others have bled for. Now the achievement is "Christianity's own." One could go on and on.

131

Soul: We will indeed go on and on. Meantime I'll begin by conceding all degrees and intensities of martyrdom, sacrifice, and costly grace, to many outside as well as inside the orbit of faith. Surpassing us, equaling us. And as to the second point, granted also. This is a kind of duplicity I cringe from; I admit its practice, and then some.

I: So, now what? Where does that leave us?

Soul: It pushes my argument along, which truly isn't meant as an argument at all, but as an attempt to touch on sources and resources, symbols, contrasting histories.

I: Go on. It's so nice to meet a reasonably uncontentious spirit these days.

Soul: I'll try, so help me. What strikes me first of all about Jesus and Marx, they're like every other ikon, hero. They get assimilated, ground into the world's systems; which are, of course, older than they, and simply pick them up and sweep them along, new ballast for an old trip. Thus, a hundred years after Marx, we have Soviet imperialism and Chinese imperialism, even, God help us, Cuban imperialism. And three hundred years after Jesus, big worldly enterprise streamed along, in his name no less. Church and state, hurrah! and Jesus be damned. We make fast food of our heroes, or hero sandwiches. They're meant to help the army, as Napoleon said, to "march on its belly," a full belly to be sure. And an army to be sure.

I: That's all well and good, but hardly to the point, which I thought was something like "sacrificial love," a hallmark of Christians.

Soul: I was trying to clear the air, get back to sources. We have two unfulfilled claims to be embarrassed about, you and I. The trouble is not unfinished revolutions. Talk of that only loads the issue, as though it was ever the intention of second and third generation Christians or Marxists to push a revolution along. What we have in Christianity and Marxism is something else again; aborted revolutions. The state, far from withering away in favor of a declassified people, is now as inflated as Gargantua's belly, and marches its belly into Afghanistan, among other places.

I: And how about the church, and that famous second Coming?

Soul: You know it as well as I, but you're going to make me eat crow. So here goes. The church baptized the emperor, a purportedly holy act. But what it was in fact doing was pouring water on the fires of Pentecost. One Coming was quite enough for the church, one Coming at a time. And we settled down to the king's table, put the truth tellers out the door, like Lazarus. Let them eat crow. Thus was aborted the second Coming. Thus the new covenant was annulled by a newer one. Now we no longer had "sacrificial love" at center stage, we had the grand inquisitor. He knew how to dispose of our lingering embarrassment, a ragged beggar at the door, named (no one quite knew his name) Lazarus or Christ or someone. But in any case, who cared?

I: Someone cared. A few cared. Don't oversimplify.

Soul: You're right, someone cared. But in one case, they get shipped out of Moscow, and in another, they're told to clam up on infallibility or the ordination of women, or—

I: This thing is still far from clear. What are you getting at about sacrificial love and Christians? Could you get to the point, if you have one? You've already admitted something even a seeing-eye dog can see, that heroes and martyrs and Christlike figures are by no means a Christian invention. Now what?

Soul: Now this. What Christians are *called* to. Not just a calling to live well, decently, inwardly, faithfully. But a calling to give ourselves to all lives, indeed to all life.

I: But how does that differ from the call issued to any decent person, the call echoing in the inner ear of the newly born—or maybe even the twice born, when they're not stone deaf? No one, I take it, is entirely ignorant of what a human being is, seeing that most of us live in a common skin, in the same world. . . .

Soul: Against all odds, and going out on the longest limb of the tallest tree of the forest—I'd say, Christians are called not only to give their lives, they're called to take no one's life. For whatever reason.

I: You call that unique? I call it the common touch of the spirit: Hindu, Buddhist, Jewish. Human.

Soul: Agreed. I call it faithful, in a scriptural sense. I mean a true scripture, a revelation.

I: A revelation. You realize, of course, that any kook in a corner can claim a revelation, and most do. A revelation that can even tell the kook to kill someone—for Christ.

Soul: You're being funny, about as funny as a hangman tripping the trap. But I'd say seriously, if the revelation is for real, it'll read: Thou shalt not kill.

I: So now you're telling God how to play God.

Soul: No, just hoping God will be Himself.

I: And until He is, you won't listen?

Soul: Exactly. Listen, I take it that if God wants to say something to us, it ought to dovetail with what He's already said to us.

I: And what was that?

Soul: Consult the famous four, M, M, L, J.

I: I have. It's not all that clear.

Soul: Maybe you're illiterate.

I: Thanks a lot.

Soul: I'm quite serious. Outside the circle, which for want of a better name, someone calls the geography of faith, the New Testament takes on the more or less attractive, more or less repulsive, more or less persuasive look of any ideology being pushed anywhere. An ideology, always, more or less.

I: "More or less." As contrasted with what?

Soul: As contrasted with "This is It." Or, as Chesterton called it: The Thing.

I: You're now being opaque, more or less.

Soul: Not really. Or not intentionally. I mean something quite simple. An ideology can win assent, even set feet in motion, even create martyrs; if it offers more rather than less. A faith, on the other hand, can offer—only what it offers, an ikon. Or as the Christians used to say, "a way." Ideology, by the way, was brought to a peak of perfection by the Greeks, an embodied noble way of being in the world, of piercing the veil of the invisible, of coping tragically. It was all immensely persuasive and ennobling.

Then, I'm sorry to say, some obscure rabbi threw sand in the well-meshed gears. Some equally obscure zealot came along, saw the wreckage, and lived to describe it. He wrote, "It's all up with Greek wisdom."

I: Said he. On what occasion?

Soul: Well, you see, if I may be pardoned the expression, he'd had a revelation. Word had gotten around about a dead man who stood up again, and was beating at the door.

I: Saying what?

Soul: Saying, among other things, that killing possibly wasn't the most enlightened application of Greek wisdom. Adding that killing for God's sake was, if possible, an even worse idea. So would folk, Christian folk, cease and desist. As of now. Or better still, refuse to aid and abet.

I: I remember the episode. But I think your translation of things is far less clear. I don't recall, moreover, that the trashing of Greek wisdom has had any large impact on things to come; things which disastrously and visibly, have already come. Including wars innumerable, pogroms, holocausts, Hiroshima, and our own nuclearized culture and lives.

Soul: I'd be a fool to claim any large impact. Maybe any small impact as well. I was insisting (insisting? it's a little like pissing into the prevailing wind)—insisting we get back to sources, see how this so-called sacrificial love got started. At the beginning I find a few people who don't mind dying for good reasons. And, like our own obscure rabbi, they become not so obscure. Because they wouldn't stay dead.

I: Not to stay dead doesn't strike me as a very locomotive idea.

Soul: You're being facetious. But more, you positively disappoint me. You haven't even brought up the worst news of all, the news that all but stops me in my tracks.

I: Namely?

Soul: Namely this. The same West that imported and indigenized Christ, that colonized Him abroad, that industrialized Him at home, that fed Him through all the conduits and images of its culture, that sent missionaries about the world to say how good was the good news, that plagiarized and satirized and idolized Him, the West that held Him briefly at center eye, in this or that ragtag saint or deviant or heretic, the West that crusaded for Him and hit the road and the seven seas for Him, that killed in His name and baptized in His name and broke His bread and broke His bones—the same West that captures Him in its mosaics and murals and domes (and claims Him through draft exemptions and tax exemptions)—why, this same West is now manning most of the world's bunkers, is arguably the great *agent provocateur* of the last day. I don't hesitate to say that the civilization that created Christendom has now, in the space of thirty-five years, created a nuclear anti-Christ.

I: Thank you. Then you concede that my skepticism is well-founded. That the Christian ideal of sacrificial love is as dead as the dodo's doppelgänger. Or that it never existed at all, in the sense of a social force, a fulcrum, a way of turning history around.

Soul: Take it easy. You don't have to leap in like that for the kill. Where's your sacrificial love?

I: That's not our topic, as the scholars say. We're into the *idea* of sacrificial love. That's our "field." And in any case, you haven't gotten close to my objection, so well stated by yourself. So let's hear you answer you.

Soul: Let me muse a while. Sacrificial love, universal death. Christ reqires an anti-Christ, in the nature of things. The holy Spirit requires an unholy spirit, also in the nature of things. To affirm the one is not to deny the other. In fact, I'd be willing to venture that the denial of one is effectively the denial of the other. Thus, our best evidence for the existence of demons is, not the demons, who are great liars and would make dupes of us all, especially by denying they exist, swearing they do not exist, on couches and in board rooms and classrooms and pulpits and media, all those dank places of the spirit where lies creep up, lay claim, feed off us. But our best evidence for the existence of demons, is One who loved the truth greatly; who, moreover, fought the demons to the finish.

I: All this talk about the "nature of things" floors me. Too static. In any case, I don't like your dualism. To me, things are far simpler, more stark. History keeps casting ashore a certain number of biological sports, every millennium or so; if we're lucky, every century or so. They shake the sea water from their eyes, wander about, gather a few fratelli about them; legends spring up, fioretti get written, a number of the starry-eyed get themselves killed, tossed back in the sea for bait. And the tide rolls in again. And, if we're lucky, we come on their fioretti, noble debris, scrolls sealed in jars. And that's all, that's all.

Soul: Who's being static now? You're trying to describe with a dead image something living, something in our midst, something without which you and I and everyone else would indeed be little more than your beloved debris of history.

I: Then what happens when static meets static? The noise level goes up, but where's the sense?

Soul: Let's try not to talk static. I'm thinking rather of how tough it is to find a meeting ground, even with the best of wills. Half of me is with you, half of you with me. But the other half of both of us! Those halves lie outside the ellipse, they refuse to meet, even to meet each other's eyes. There they stand, that "you" and "I," that divided self, wandering the world, outside the orbit of truth. So what is there to say, how can the two be healed, be one?

I: I'll speak for one side of the shadowy half. I've already spoken for it. I said your talk about sacrificial love is talk about debris. It doesn't signify in the land of the living. Your religion is necrophilic, it's a taxidermist's job.

Soul: There you go again, and here I come again, judgment for judgment. Let me say only, you miss a great deal. You can't imagine one half of yourself, talking the way you do. You miss the myth-making self, the clay-and-kiln self, the ikon, the poet, the harper.

I: That's a lot of halves for one whole.

Soul: Indeed, they're all halves of a soul that you partition or cut up, to your grief. And let me revert to your original image, almost your original sin, the Christian as debris of history. Let me suggest that in the two millennia since Christ and the four millennia since the Buddha, tides have cast up other debris than the dead shells of believers.

I: Like what?

Soul: Like the debris of kingdoms. Which is to say, if loving sacrifice hasn't worked well, hateful killing hasn't served its practitioners well either. I mean even by their own criterion of "well" and "badly."

I: What criteria?

Soul: Their own survival. Their dream, the dream of mandarins and shahs and juntas and emperors and pharaohs. The dream of immortality, the dream of the running dogs, and—But you know all this.

I: Even admitting all that, where does it leave us?

Soul: Maybe with this: Give or hoard, kill or be killed, fight to the finish or fall to knee. You take your choice. And you don't choose in the dark. And you don't choose alone. Someone has chosen, and His choice was on our behalf; that the half might be whole.

As Pascal said long ago, you make your wager.

IV

Of Priests, Women,
Women Priests,
and Other
Unlikely Recombinants

They seemed so macho, self-assured, American. They come at me in public like members of a prosecutor's team. I was a suspect in the Matter of the Jesuits v. Berrigan, a case as hopeless of outcome as Jarndyce v. Jarndyce, as unwinnable, a stalemate. Within the club, one had betrayed the rules.

Brothers in Christ? Well, sort of. But it went otherwise when the Jesuit novices appeared in the audience of a public lecture. During the discussion, they took over with a vengeance. "Hadn't I written the following . . . ?" "What were my current views on the church, and the Jesuits?" The tone was high and mighty, they were sniffing out a heterodox, possibly a heretic.

It was chilling, it was educative. One knew at such a time, and winced at the knowledge, that the future was the past. They would go their way, I would go mine. There was no point in dreaming of a new generation, new outlook, culturally free, on the move. This had not been born, it had not even been imagined.

◁ ○ ▷

You have to taste life before you can celebrate life. This seems plain fact on the face of it. But what to make of all those liturgical experts who, year after year, gather to tell one and all what motions to go through, and when and why, around the cold altars?

◁ ○ ▷

The dominant mood, in public and private, in church and state, is something deeper than depression; a stupefaction. People go in circles, blank-faced. There are no maps. In consequence, many plod along in the old track, interminably. Or they go where they are forbidden to go. The old taboos fall in the name of freedom, sexual or psychological, a kind of mauve-scented slavery. And Big Bro grins his wolfish grin.

◁ ○ ▷

When I came out of jail in 1972, almost everyone was sporting new haircuts and new clothes. It all happened in my absence, the Jesuits had gotten "liberated." I must confess to having had no part in this, either as newborn babe or as midwife. Alas, to be apart from a transaction that, by all reports, was momentous, biggest and best! Jesuits now had their own money, their own cars, they were free to be free. So it all went. Pardon me, it looked like death.

Then, to go along with the wardrobes and hair blowers, there was a new jargon. Discernment, group therapy, directed retreats, gimme space. . . . The theologians were tweedy as racoons, smoking away like Ivy League *arrivistes,* all bonhommie and officers-club back slaps. Teilhard was in, contention and claims were out. Everything wore the misty look of pre-dawn pollution, you had to grope your way among the gurus and groupies. Where was I? The kingdom, they said, welcome to the kingdom. The hell you say, said I.

◁ ○ ▷

It seemed to be working. Then you probed a bit, and there were the same old dry bones under the chic taxidermy. Superiors were still in the catbird seat, they hadn't given over an iota of power, of investments, of holding the line against marriage, women, gays. Had anything happened? A cultural camouflage. A certain easing over into the culture, in the name of something called church renewal. We now belonged. At the Protestant faculties, at the prestige universities. We were indeed riding first class. On the Titanic.

◁ ○ ▷

The Jesuits are masters of invention. They come out of the culture, they know how to take its pulse, try its winds and trim their sails. Nothing extravagant, nothing ahead of its time, nothing too fast. Consensus, consensus!

And then, of course, the institutional connection. We're not running the Little Brothers of Jesus, we're not running the Catholic Worker. Manifestly. We're running Georgetown University, the School of Foreign Service, we're a nursery for the State Department, only the brightest and best get born here. So connections are everything, dollars are nearly everything. The Shah of Iran, Kissinger, are good dollar connections. Therefore . . .

◁ ○ ▷

The only Jesuits who look me up or want to talk seriously are by and large third world types, beats, people in personal turmoil at the misdirection, misfirings, injustices, concrete impasse of things. I can't offer them much except a certain wry skill in surviving the Sillys on Stilts. I'm still around; not much more.

◁ ○ ▷

Women who want to enter the priesthood, or who are already ordained, have at least some inkling of the stalemate within the ranks. The truth of being woman is a good boot camp for being a nobody; in culture, in church. And "nobody," "non-person" is a good definition of a priest today, female or male, given both church and culture. Properly, soberly understood. Some say the scripture says that's where we belong.

I was invited to a seminary class on liberation theology. They had agreed on two truths; violence in the third world was acceptable, indeed inevitable; and a Marxist economic analysis was crucial. I didn't like either idea, and said so. It seemed to me that a Marxist analysis was old hat, that the West was as post-Marxist as it was post-capitalist. And that third world violence was as unacceptable to Christians as was first or second or fourth or any other.

I could read the response in their eyes. I had broken a taboo, as sacred as a first commandment of the left. Naïve, jejune, I'd lost again.

◁ ○ ▷

A nonperson. You don't signify. They look you over, you don't meet acceptable standards. Or the big boys meet, make big decisions, plans, projections. You aren't invited. Or rather, you're disinvited. World without end.

◁ ○ ▷

Priesthood? One could huff and puff about mystery, sacrament, sign, moments of grace. These I take to be realities. I am also consoled that they are out of our grasp, control, consuming.

◁ ○ ▷

And this is the Day of the Consumer. The Day of Seizure; Don't Forget It. Above all, don't forget it, women. The caste implications, the control units, are humming. If you come in and join up, the machos will know how to deal with that too. Which is to say, the penal implications of the penis ought not be misread. To be deprived is to be a "case," a patient, a freak, an example. It is To Be Dealt With.

◁ ○ ▷

When something is working badly for those it was designed to work for, what solution? Commonly, culturally speaking, do more of the same. Multiplied mistakes cancel out the initial mistake; the sublime illogic. What then to say to women who want to join the Early Mistake? Mistaken identity? One has to think of starting over. But whether women can correct the massive and multiplied misservices of the Hippos on High— this seems to be matter for valid questioning.

◁ ○ ▷

We do well in a bad time not to multiply the "bads." Men I respect in the priesthood aren't particularly happy in thinking male. They feel miserable under the weight of life today, just as women do. That "just as" needs, of course, to be treated carefully; women are outside, men in, and the difference is not slight.

At the same time, it's worth saying that spite gets us nowhere. And on the question of priesthood, the "in" male and the "out" female meet on a ground that's fairly familiar to each; one barely making it meets another not making it.

◁ o ▷

To say that life isn't offering a great deal to any of us doesn't heal the long-untended wounds.

A better beginning might be the common admission of a common plight, male and female, in the effort to be faithful to a human vocation; violation, insult, jail, the beetling brow of the law. Each has the right to kick and scream until we have (1) a common share of our common patrimony (matrimony)—which certainly includes equal access to ministry, pulpit, sacraments, right up to bishoprics and papal tiaras (for those who feel called to such bric-a-brac), and (2) a vote on where and how our lives get lived, used, spent, given away.

◁ o ▷

Access to the mysteries, the good news made both good and new. Need I tell anyone we are being drowned in bad news; certainly bad, hardly new? I think on the contrary, good news waits on women; I think it waits on men. It waits on each of us, reborn.

◁ o ▷

Please don't wash us in hog wash. A big case is made in anti-woman-priest polemics of the huge shift in symbols required if women are to stand at the altar. This is, to say the least, reading history through the rearview mirror. Such "scholarship" is always late, always after the fact, invariably in service to special interests. It loves to act as though—Why, look, we just arbitrarily happen to occupy the catbird seat! We're those wide-eyed innocents, open to every contrary wind, nothing on our minds except disinterested service of the truth. . . . Thus, the scholars become apologists, indifferent to injustice; and the apologists become ideologues. They prefer historical jousting to a simple look at manifest injustice. A fascist stalling tactic.

◁ ○ ▷

In such matters, it helps to stay with a few simple ideas, and see where they lead. But some critics make history (in this case, male history, a bad start) into an obstacle against a better human arrangement. They also mistrust people, including their fellow Christians; the majority of whom do not sit in endowed university chairs announcing the facts of life to those "below." (A little like lifeguards scanning the beaches from chairs the height of the Empire State building.)

Would Christians accept the ministry of women alongside men? My experience is that good will is available; people adjust quickly, even with excitement, to new arrangements, especially when these are presented as forms of requital, righting of wrongs. "How sensible, I never thought of that before" is a common reaction in such matters, from the pew or the church door. But in the pulpit or podium, the process is infinitely more tortuous, the minds out of touch.

◁ ○ ▷

Ours was a church of outsiders from the start. This is often said. The implications are just as often ignored or sidestepped; because the "outside" character of our beginnings is, of course, taught by insiders.

◁ ○ ▷

Still, cold comfort is better than none, considering current shortages. We might consider Jesus; who, it could be argued, is still shivering at the doorway of this or that sublime chancel. He cannot be washed hands of, He will not go away. A perpetual embarrassment to grand and petty inquisitors alike.

In all this, it won't do to comfort ourselves with, "Well, in any case, it's psychiatrically verified that sons (daughters) always kick out the old man in order to come into their own. . . ."

Their own? The old man? Jesus didn't come on, in the first place, as big daddy at all; but as defenseless, otherworldly, an artisan, a worker, a friend, a wanderer, a random cast really, empty of hand and pocket, a nonbelonger and nonjoiner.

It seems to follow; all who wish to meet Him must do so on His ground. He won't come in. Won't be assimilated. A Jew is a Jew, take it or leave it. You want to meet Him? step outside, into the dark. But who wants to hear such talk?

◁ o ▷

There's little doubt that when the Gospels got written, people leaned quirkily, stormily on charisms, resonances, right speech, a passion to serve, the ictus that went further than plod, on wisdom and wisdom's outreach. And not to forget in a spineless time—courage, raw as a wound. Jail experience, savvy, street smarts. The range of the eye was wider then, the understanding more worldly, they had more news to call good. Passion was in the air, firm claims, symbols pushed hard. It was faith erupting into history, not airlifted; the underground was surfacing, hot lava.

That passion shaped us. But then we cooled. People once died for beliefs (killed others, too). But we come swaddled in something called security, dogma, from cradle clothes to shroud. And who today dies for anything at all, anyone at all? We don't die "for"; we die "of"; decline and fall. The martyr is now the patient.

◁ o ▷

People are hung high, wavering between a tradition gone sour, and new starts that peter out fast. Are we stuck at the dead end of a once useful and pleasing thing? and stuck there, can we do no better than improvise, hearsay, catch what we can? Somewhere in a middle ground we would like to stand and walk together, sensible connections holding fast, a measure of verve and spontaneity. Alas, the path is narrow, like the walkway above a tank of piranas. . . .

◁ o ▷

I believe we were created for ecstasy. And redeemed for it, at considerable cost. Certain vagrant unrepeatable moments of life tell us this, if we will but attend. Such moments, moreover, are clues to the native structure and texture of things. Not merely are such glorious fits and starts meant to "keep us going," a fairly unattractive idea, but ecstasy fuels and infuses us from the start, is our proper distillation and energy of soul. One could dream the world, the poet says, and one could even dream the eye; but who can imagine the act of seeing? We will never have enough of this, we will never have done with it.

◁ ○ ▷

If, tomorrow or the day after, women stood toe-to-heel with men at the altars of the church, and in the pulpits—what then? Would we have the same old church? We would probably have the same old world.

And that, in the old phrase, ought to give pause.

If all those destructive cuts and thrusts had been parried, healed in Christ, as Paul says they were meant to; if all those divisions and hatreds and put-downs (a few of which Paul helped along, on the side)—if these disappeared tomorrow, and if this vanishing of the old disorder were made clear beyond doubt, were reflected in service, worship, office, dignity—why, what then? We would probably have the same old world.

Probably. But at least one element of that world, an element which thinks of itself as drawn forth from that world, differing from that world, opposed to that world's rule and conduct—at least that element, that yeast, that little flock, that tight-knit unfearing witnessing knot of troublemakers—at least these would have once spoken and been heard, would be something to turn to; relief, solace, ikon. Would (take it or leave it) be something else than the fitful, selfish, death-ridden world. And in this sense the world would no longer be the same. It would have lost all claim over us.

◁ ○ ▷

There is nothing more crushing, in fact, and more revolting to the moral nostril, than a church that ignores the outcry of the disenfranchised. We've all suffered under it, the sense of nightmarish unreality, a wound at the heart of things. Let the world act in such a way, let the megacorporations or the armed forces or the state departments act this way; it is the way of the world, dog-eat-dog, devil take the hindmost. But what shall we do, what is to become of us, when this mechanized, macho spirit infests the church and turns on us? We go hoarse, talking to statuary with chipped ears; we lose spirit, we give up. And we bring home bad news, too often for our own good; we wear the look of those who believe the worst.

The lucky ones (my own luck is good) find a few friends who help cut the knots, free up the soul. Who try, as best we may, to do good work ourselves; that news gets around.

$$\triangleleft \ o \ \triangleright$$

Anger is good fuel, but must we always be angry? conservation, occasion.

$$\triangleleft \ o \ \triangleright$$

Every attempt to "spiritualize" a simple human difficulty ends up looking spurious, ludicrous. Witness the hauling out of high-minded altruistic arguments—all in a bad cause. What is wondrously concealed by the huffings, puffings, and pieties, are the underlying (not so far under at that) class interests that batten off such nonsense. Instead of a quite simple question; who shall have power, who shall not? But not a word of this. The lofty Himalayan air breathed by our authorities! and it is all rounded off with an appeal to obedience, to clinch matters. Alienating, destructive.

$$\triangleleft \ o \ \triangleright$$

The healing of the woman bent double, in Luke 13. Nuanced and delightful. I cannot, for the life of me, find anyone who treats it adequately; so here goes a try.

She was bent over, Luke says (and he ought to know) by a diabolic spirit. Could it be that she was fated to dramatize in her frame, the fate of women in that culture (in every culture)? No one says so. Males write history, generally; then to place things beyond reasonable doubt, they write a male commentary. But

Luke steps aside from all that; or better, Jesus does. In freedom, He walks over those puerile taboos. He takes the initiative with the woman; "He called her" to Him when He saw her condition. Then He "laid His hands upon her." And simply announced her cure. She straightened up. And "she praised God." How sublime! A woman bent double (bent doubly) under the burden of hideous culture and worse religion, is healed of this evil spirit. For "a spirit" is at work in her, not a disease; more accurately, a diseased spirit. The culture, the religion, are rightly regarded by Jesus as demonic. The woman must be exorcised, of culture, of religion. Then she stands upright, then with all her wit and will, she responds to God. Can you see her face at that moment?

The keepers of the status quo are, of course, outraged. If we know anything, we know why. The miraculous is of no account to them. Religion is business. The rule is business as usual. Business is good.

But something deeper than this is in question; the healing of—a woman. Her face, alight with hope and joy, is an affront to their consecrated gloom, the atmosphere of a sanctuary which is no more than a counting house.

Would they have struck back with such irrational fury had a man been healed under the same circumstances? One is allowed to doubt it. In any case, Jesus is at pains to note that He has liberated, not a man, but a "daughter of Abraham." This is her dignity. He refers to it, against all custom. A daughter of Abraham stands, upright; stands up, as we say, for her rights.

In the gospel the title is unique, where "sons of Abraham" abound. In the Jewish Bible, the title is unthinkable. But no commentator notes these things, as far as I can find.

◁ ○ ▷

I wish someone could draw us out of trivia.

I wish someone could draw us out of trauma.

I wish someone could help us get sane, or stay sane.

I wish someone could cleanse and heal our eyesight, help us turn our heads away from non-questions, false questions, destructive questions. I mean the questions that a straight-faced, strait-jacketed culture keeps pushing like crazy. Like, how many millions can we kill and still get away with it. Or, why not a bit more experimentation on prisoners? Or, let's go back to capital punishment, that'll show those muggers, crooks, killers, once and for all. Or, let's pare down the welfare system, too many chiselers. Or, let's sell the latest lethal toys on both sides of a border dispute; that way, we get the buck and they get the bang. Or, let's get massive abortion going, there's not enough food and housing and jobs around for people (which is to say, for us, for ourselves)—let alone for the unborn. . . .

◁ ○ ▷

One woman I know has sat in and been arrested at both abortion clincs and the Pentagon. Thus enraging someone in both places. Her crime; an integrated conscience.

◁ ○ ▷

To make it in radical circles in America you're supposed to carry about an annotated list of correct attitudes and causes, conformed to stereotype. Thus, toward the end of the Vietnam war, one was "supposed" to be anti-war. At that point it was a position that could hardly be called radical or threatened. It was plain chic. You were (are) also supposed to be pro-abortion; supposed, that is, in the expectation of the left. Your ethical choices are rather presupposed than supposed; that is to say, prepackaged and pushed by social pressures.

I well remember the fury that greeted me when I broke this mold, suggesting publicly that one was required to defend and foster life along its whole spectrum, prebirth to last gasp. Clearly, this talk is intolerable. A whole thicket of misunderstandings arises. In the above case, one is immediately tarred with the brush of bad faith; of a church which is certainly in bad faith; madly anti-abortion, madly attached to war.

You start extricating yourself, as best you might.

Then there are the iniquities of a social system that refuses abortion monies to poor women, while the rich may cut and slice in perfect or near perfect safety, anonymity. You try to make clear the injustice of that. You try, moreover, to point out the horrors of a system that can do no better for its citizens than grant equal access to the death of the unborn. Even as the same machinery moves, with icy singleness, to plan the death of practically everyone.

But who grasps the unity of social method here, the linkages? Death is the solution to every human impasse; death and more death.

◁ ○ ▷

One woman accuses me of making a "war on women." An irony that might be called delicious if it weren't so painful.

But I call abortion a war on the unborn.

◁ ○ ▷

The question of alternatives today. People ask, with varying degrees of despair, where they might go. The question is all the more grievous, voiced as it is by people of stature, merit, intelligence; who love the church, long to give of their lives. And they witness the imbecility, connivance, wheeling, base politics, neglect of the poor, defamation of Christ's spirit. Where to go, when in good conscience one can hardly bear to stay? Up till recently, it was publicly titillating, a "story," news, when one "left the church." Now the meaning of the phrase is clouded, the announcement brings a yawn.

Part of the trouble is that so few who walked out landed anywhere. Frying pan to fire; they left the church and the culture swallowed them whole. It seems better, as a rule, to hang around where one was born, trying as best one may to make it with a few friends, to do what one can in the common life: instead of launching out in the wilds, by and large wilder than the church.

Unless, of course, there is manifest injustice going on. In which case, one is advised to take chances, yell loud and clear; then, as a last resort, walk out yelling. (But have a landing pad as well as a launching pad!)

But the weight is in favor of hanging on, I think.

◁ ○ ▷

I'm struck that the women are battering at the church doors, just when everything in church and culture is announcing an "end of things." Not the end of the world, maybe (though that could be argued too). But certainly the end of the culture as we know it, as we were born into it, and came to self-understanding by resisting it. . . .

◁ o ▷

Women have always washed corpses and prepared them for burial. Women are in charge of delivery rooms—in more ways than one. A metaphor for today? Women make the death decent and the birth possible.

◁ o ▷

Sunday at St. Stephen's in Washington. This is one of very few parishes that take in street people during the cruel winter months, house and feed them. They also welcome the peace community from Jonah House, offer a place to pray and plan the continuing presence there. So it was quite natural and moving and befitting that I be invited to preach; a homecoming.

The Eucharist was conducted by women. And they invited me to serve Communion, along with several others. Black, white, young, old; and women orchestrating, setting the tone, announcing with authority, reverence, and verve, the Lord's body and blood.

It was overwhelming. (Most worship today is crashingly underwhelming.) It was like a quiet expedition of a few friends to the other side of the moon, from this clamorous and polluted side. *Solvitur ambulando.* The absurd sexist knot of the centuries, tightened by macho muscle and muddle, was cut.

And all so naturally. The children wandered quietly about, folk prayed, talked up, sang, took Communion. No one seemed to think that anything of moment, beyond the sublime faith and hope that were on the air, was taking place. I wondered if a big stir would have gone through us if Jesus had walked through the chancel door. I doubt it.

How did all this come about, how did great changes get proposed, accepted, even rejoiced at? One could note the absence of hyperpsychologizing, expertise, sensitivity sessions, expensive gurus, hot and heavy breathing, shrinkification, touchy feely follies, inflations of spirit—that plague of self-indulgence. No, the people met with their pastor, they prayed together, struggled, things were worked through.

One notes something else. Liturgy here is no fetish or idol; the god is not fed on the hour or enshrined. The same parish that welcomes women ministers feeds and houses the homeless and hungry. The same parish also blesses and helps those who prepare for nonviolence at the Pentagon, in defense of life. The main business of the parish is not maintaining a nest, womb, space station, esthetic cave for the middle class. It is stewardship and service, up close, day-after-day, blow hot, blow cold. Such conduct, I think, accords with, and confers sanity.

Thus, what might be considered audacious or innovative elsewhere, is taken for granted here. People had the look of those who work at their faith, sweat it out. And the media were absent. Two good signs.

◁ ○ ▷

Today, despair is utterly rational; one can offer perfectly plausible reasons why it flourishes in everyone's better home and garden. Beginning with this one: Made in America. Hope, on the other hand, offers no reason for its existence. It has no goals, no five-year plans, no assurance it will be around tomorrow. It is (like God) essentially useless. Hope will not ease life or make money while you sleep; it is neither an energy pill nor a (nonaddictive) sleep inducer.

Despair is a cultural conclusion, deductive. Anyone can own one; time payments easily arranged. Read the clock on the cover of the Bulletin of Atomic Scientists, the stockmarket report, the rising index of food costs, the—Worse; go hungry, go homeless, go unwanted, go to hell.

Hope is something else; a gift, Paul calls it, a grace. Its highest expression is an irony; "hoping against hope." You take all the reasons for giving up, you admit their weight, you grant all their crushing power, you wince and cry out—then you toss them off your back. And you go on.

I write these lines while Philip is in jail once more, a six-month sentence for blood-pouring at the Pentagon. May marked the anniversary of Catonsville. Philip has served over four years in jail for speaking truth to power. Has the country changed, has anything changed? Have people struck out on a new path, are they giving a new example? The questions seem to me an invitation to despair. The proper answer is, things are worse than ever.

But that's beside the point. The point of hope; which is; Philip has been faithful, so have our friends. So would I be. Hope on!

V

Finally—
I Pledge Allegiance
to Forty-Seven Graffiti:
A Declaration
of Dependence

1. Don't be afraid to be afraid or appalled to be appalled. How do you think the redwoods feel these days, or the whales, or, for that matter, most humans?

2. Generally speaking, when asked to speak, be silent; when asked to shut up, accede on the instant.

3. Keep your soul to yourself. (Soul is a possession worth paying up for, they're growing rarer.) Know that there is practically no public speech worth agreeing with or lingering over. Monks have a secret worth knowing.

4. When you go to jail, the first rule is "survive." When you're outside, the rule is roughly the same. As to the details of the formula, I don't know. No one knows. But it's useful to keep trying.

5. If you want to live for a while, do so. If you want to die, do so. Don't heed those who weaken you in either task, urging you to "carry on." Mostly, they want you around for a substitute, a mask, or a main dish.

6. As to your religion also, the rule is useful: keep your mouth shut. It's no one's business, pure effrontery, like: "describe your wife's body."

7. When asked to go public, go private. When possible, escape to the redwoods. When impossible, put up with things. Knowing ruefully that you asked for it.

8. About practically everything in the world, there's nothing you can do. This is Socratic wisdom, pressure on the fulcrum Archimedes never came on. However. About a few things you can do something. Do it, with a good heart.

9. We're in the era of busted banjos, all their strings sprung. Plunk away at one string. Better a backstoop single-string plunker than a mute inglorious Milton.

10. Do what you want to do, often. Do what you don't want to do, just as often. "Often" is the word to watch. Watching it, wants and non-wants stay in place, which is secondary.

11. Call on Jesus when all else fails. Call on Him when all else succeeds. As to the second, *caveas*. (Except that it never happens anyway.)

12. Most people are carnivorous. This is more than a casual observation. They don't want you on the program, they want you on the menu.

13. Vegetarians who eat in vegetarian restaurants are generally dull, if not dour. In a meat restaurant you can order coffee if you're scrupulous, and at least hear a guffaw or two or meet someone wacky or someone who likes you.

14. If one's bent is breaking the law, there's very little anyone else can do to prevent it—or should do—friends included. In any case, you'll meet interesting folk and get to bunk down with them for a period. Bring along a toothbrush.

15. Likewise, on a long drive, there's bound to be a dull stretch or two. Don't go anywhere with someone who expects you to be interesting indefinitely. And don't be merciless on fellow passengers in this regard. Try hard to smile after a coffee stop. As to destination, be glad if you get there.

16. If it's a long ride, pay something. If a short one, hum along.

17. Practically no one has the stomach to love you if you don't love yourself. They just endure. So do you.

18. Now and again, after you've performed well (or badly), pat yourself on the back. It's easy, imagine you're an ambulatory octopus, close your eyes and reach around. I find this a great help when things are going so well, or so badly, that my hair stands up.

19. Start with the impossible. Proceed calmly toward the improbable. There are at least five fire exits.

20. At a weekend conference, some Irish peace women and I sneaked a drink. It wasn't death we were trying to get around, it was the conference. There's a clue here I'll have to think about.

21. The thing the Christians call the cross. In antiquity we're told there was someone on it. In Italy, I was shown a cross a seventeenth-century missionary had carried about. It opened up into a stiletto. Something weird here; adaptation, degradation. It's called either-or religion, nothing to do with Kierkegaard.

22. If one uses big words to cloud simple truths, the Bible, though open, stays closed. The purported virtue of this method is, you never have to say: "Let's tell the truth to one another, and see what happens."

23. If your first thoughts are revolting or hateful, try some second thoughts. They usually improve on the former ones.

24. Here's the way it goes in America: they drive people mad, then they put them together again. Thus the product of psychiatry is pure America. Detroit does the same thing to cars; mad driving, crackup, now and again you can patch them up for another try.

25. You have to be a little insane to avoid going totally bananas today. In new acquaintances, I always listen for the ding-dong of the bell-buoy; most of the time, it's cracked. But now and again, a true note strikes—this one can ride the rough seas.

26. "Politics as ultimate reality"; the ultimate blasphemy. It's also a clue as to why Marxists, including the American Christian kind, don't cotton to me.

27. As to imagination, most of us can't even imagine it. Not merely its function, but its existence. This is the triumph of the super cog machine. If we can come on the uses and misuses of the imagination, we have come on an alternative, a way of (a) not being ground up, and (b) not grinding others up. But this is still pre-imaginative. To push matters, what are we to do with our lives?

28. Psychologizing of experience. One way or another, it usually goes hand in hand with sexualizing of experience. But clearly there are experiences which are neither sexual nor psychological, even reductively. Otherwise, the culture is a kind of loose noose around the neck. Loose, since capital punishment isn't for the likes of us. But a noose nonetheless, a silken one. Like a Gucci cravat.

29. You get beyond Number 28 by getting off the "couch culture." It's called healing. The gospels tell us it was Jesus' specialty: "take up your couch and walk."

30. You say you're sick? I say the shrinks have flayed you alive. But to live in the world, you have to have a skin.

31. The more insistent a "sell" becomes, the more it appears as a simple con job, a heist. This is true of Marxist salvation theory, of peaceable uses of the atom, of bomb shelters, of shrinkification cures, of behavior modification, of . . . There just aren't that many saviors around, the economy being thin, the market hardly bullish.

32. When everything has a penis implication, there's very little left to be sensuous or warm-hearted about. The first leads inevitably to know-how, technique, a horror. The second, to the ripe grapevine, the oven of creation. Picasso vs. Van Gogh.

33. The expressions "waging war," "wages of war," imply both cost and reward. One pays up, often in blood, one is sometimes rewarded—with a gilded dog-tag. But what about waging the peace? What are we to pay, what are the costs, who

comes across with them, what are the rewards? People don't ordinarily take to this, it's a new language. Or we get it only from a war footing, a war history. Then we start desperately poking about in the dark, e.g., trying to establish a "peace academy" as a counter to the military colleges. A little like carting a wax image of Christ into hell.

34. In Eden, people were told to eat, invited to gaze, and commanded not to consume. It was a reasonable scheme of things. We know it now, perhaps too late. We are now unable simply to gaze, our eyes have tentacles. And we have lost the crucial difference between eating and consuming. Which is one, finally, of measure, discretion. Adam and Eve ate, day after day, of the fruits of the garden: a delight. But one day they set out to consume. The first murder followed shortly, its symbol had been seized on.

35. I went up into a redwood grove to gaze. After all, living in purgatory, one deserves a smidgeon of paradise.

36. I work steadily, though in spasms. Possibly I'm at a point in life where this is valid. Having neither the health nor the discipline to shoulder my way through the thicket, like Merton, I try to keep my eyes open (often fixed in horror) and my pen uncapped. Sometimes the writing fluid is blood.

37. A Jesuit friend is gone off to a thousand-dollar-a-month seminar somewhere. I told someone of this trek, and he said, "If this is the vow of poverty, bring on the chastity!"

38. Psychologize, sexualize, helter, skelter. Only a few can read the gospel, or care to; most miss the broad human spectrum of attitudes, hopes, breakthroughs, "ways out" offered by Jesus. We make of Him one of those affluent corpses kept in vaults under perpetual care, awaiting the scientific millennium when the undead shall rise to possess the earth; stale bodies, unreal estate.

39. There are possibly worse places on earth than airports. I tend in such places to think wildly of tipped over privies, Forest Lawns, golf courses on the moon, wax museums, Fellini's rotting horses. My solution is to bite my lips and hang on,

madly summoning the four last things. An old-fashioned teaching has it that penance performed here will not be exacted elsewhere. Alleluia!

40. Airplanes. I survive by watching the movies, without earphones, reading the lips of actors. Since I understand practically nothing that is said, I feel quite at home, little different than I do aground.

41. There are two methods of surviving long flights. Lock yourself in the men's room. (This won't do for long, they come for you eventually.) Or stay in your seat. This gets tough unless you are a meditator or poet. Mercifully I'm usually able to do one or the other.

42. On Hiroshima day, I had this dream. A heap of atom bombs was put in my arms as I sat cross-legged, quietly on the floor. Suddenly the bombs were changed into round and oval loaves of bread. It was simple as that. Maybe, I thought, the dream was saying something about my vocation. Such a sublime transubstantiation might, as in the case of Jesus, require that one give his life. Not ready, by any means, but willing.

43. The times are so paltry, induce such paltriness of mind, that most of our idols are also infantile. Idolettes. We are bested by demonic children. The "big ones" are reserved for the moral giants of history, the patriarchs and matriarchs, the shapers and makers, prophets in high solitary grandeur. They wrestle, break bones, prevail; we whimper and grimace and talk of being "uncomfortable," of our "needs," of "enough space," all the degraded touchy jargon of couch and crotch.

44. Which is to say, a culture is breaking up. We cannot claim the dignity of rebirth, of a new dwelling for gods newly sprung. Our obit may read: They perished under an infestation of demonettes, like a cloud of ticks or lice. Annoyance was enough, anxiety, they died of moral acne, hemorrhoids of the spirit.

45. Not to get esoteric. The cross is folly, even to the foolish. So the equation cancels out, and the foolish "cross people,"

often working at cross purposes, often double-crossed, cross the Jordan at length.

46. They get furious when you don't "fulfill your commitments." Such messages arrive even in jail. You were supposed to be in such and such a place, talking about going to jail!—reasons why, urgency of the times, press of conscience, etc. Then instead of talking about it, from time to time one decides to do it. And this makes for anger, confusion, etc. Lesson; you are not supposed, by the rules of the academic-ecclesiastical complex, to "do it" at all. You are expected to talk about doing it.

47. A letter arrives from superiors, announcing a meeting about "communications media," our place in the public gaze, etc. It seems curiously out of tune, hyped with the more or less desperate resolve, at all price, to "get with" whatever is going on. The trouble with me is, I believe in absolutely nothing of this: that the "communications" industry communicates, that we should be producing films, etc. I see it as one huge despairing lunge toward further alienation, the old, old Jesuit trick of making it in the world. What these folk don't know is (a) that that game is long over, and (b) such a game, in any case, has nothing to do with the gospel, and (c) we will never get on the track of our true and simple work until we cast aside all such tawdry silver age pretentions. (But this sort of talk is also noncommunicating; which is the reason I set it down for my own soul. Goodbye.)